Let's Read Together

Let's Read Together

Improving Literacy Outcomes
with the
Adult–Child Interactive Reading Inventory

by

Andrea DeBruin-Parecki, Ph.D.

with invited contributors

PAUL·H·
BROOKES
PUBLISHING Co.®

Baltimore • London • Sydney

Paul H. Brookes Publishing Co.
Post Office Box 10624
Baltimore, Maryland 21285-0624

www.brookespublishing.com

Illustrations on pages 110–121 and 133 by Jane Freeman.

Manufactured in the United States of America by
Versa Press, Inc., East Peoria, Illinois.

The vignettes in this book are composites based on the authors' experiences. In most instances, names and identifying details have been changed to protect confidentiality. In all other cases, individuals' names and stories are used by permission.

Library of Congress Cataloging-in-Publication Data
DeBruin-Parecki, Andrea.
  Let's read together : improving literacy outcomes with the adult–child interactive reading inventory (ACIRI) / by Andrea DeBruin-Parecki.
      p.   cm.
  Includes bibliographical references.
  ISBN-13: 978-1-55766-762-5
  ISBN-10: 1-55766-762-4
  1. Family literacy programs—United States. 2. Reading—Parent participation—United States. 3. Home and school—United States. I. Title.

  LC151.D43 2006
  372.42'5—dc22   2006026819

British Library Cataloguing in Publication data are available from the British Library.

Contents

Contents of the CD-ROM ix
About the Author xiii
About the Contributors xv
Foreword   *Patricia A. Edwards* xvii
Acknowledgments xix

Section I   Assessment of Interactive Reading

Chapter 1   Family Literacy and Interactive Reading 3
Chapter 2   Understanding the Adult–Child Interactive Reading Inventory 19
Chapter 3   Using the Adult–Child Interactive Reading Inventory 27

Section II   Adult–Child Interactive Reading Inventory (ACIRI)

English ACIRI Tool and Scoring Sheet 41
Spanish ACIRI Tool and Scoring Sheet 43

Section III   Linked Activities to Foster Family Literacy

Category I   Enhancing Attention to Text 47
with Adam Severson

Behavior 1   Maintaining Physical Proximity 48
Class Activity: Read Aloud
"Where Did You Read with Your Child This Week?"
   Activity Sheet
Take-Home Activity: Trust Walk
Recommended Books

Behavior 2   Sustaining Interest and Attention 53
Class Activity: Telling a Story Together
Take-Home Activity: I Spy
Recommended Books

Behavior 3   Holding the Book and Turning Pages 57
   Class Activity: Mouse Hunt
   Take-Home Activity: Animals Wearing Clothing
   "Animals Should Definitely NOT Wear Clothing!"
      Activity Sheet
   Recommended Books

Behavior 4   Displaying a Sense of Audience 62
   Class Activity: Tell Me a Story
   Take-Home Activity: Making a Family Book
   Recommended Books

Category II   Promoting Interactive Reading and Supporting Comprehension 67
   with Adam Severson

Behavior 1   Posing and Soliciting Questions 68
   Class Activity: Nine Magic Wishes
   Take-Home Activity: Guess What?
   Recommended Books

Behavior 2   Identifying and Understanding Pictures and Words 72
   Class Activity: Alphabet Book
   Take-Home Activity: Riddles
   Recommended Books

Behavior 3   Relating Content to Personal Experiences 77
   Class Activity: A Terrible, Horrible, No Good, Very
      Bad Day
   Class Activity: I Like It When…
   Take-Home Activity: How We Grow
   "Memories from When I Was…" Activity Sheet
   "How I Looked…" Activity Sheet
   "Memories of What It Was Like to Be My Child's Age"
      Activity Sheet
   "How I Looked at My Child's Age" Activity Sheet
   Recommended Books

Behavior 4   Pausing to Answer Questions 86
   Class Activity: Animal Poetry
   "A Poem About an Animal" Activity Sheet
   "A Poem About Me" Activity Sheet
   "A Poem About My Family" Activity Sheet
   "A Poem from My Imagination" Activity Sheet
   Take-Home Activity: Mama, Do You Love Me?
   "A Sunny Day: A Story Filled with Questions"
      Activity Sheet
   Recommended Books

Category III   Using Literacy Strategies 97
   with Adam Severson

Behavior 1   Identifying Visual Cues 98
        Class Activity: Rebus Poems
        "Rebus Poem" Activity Sheet
        Take-Home Activity: Using Repeated Words
        "Repeated Words" Activity Sheet
        Recommended Books

Behavior 2   Predicting What Happens Next 104
        Class Activity: What Might Happen Next?
        12 "What Do You Think Is Going to Happen?" Activity Sheets
        Class Activity: Picture Walk Predictions
        "Predicting the Story" Activity Sheet
        Take-Home Activity: If You Give a Mouse a Cookie
        "Baking Cookies with Your Child" Activity Sheet
        Take-Home Activity: Can You Predict What Will Happen?
        "If You Give Someone You Love a Hug..." Activity Sheet
        Recommended Books

Behavior 3   Recalling Information 125
        Class Activity: Story Map
        "Story Map" Activity Sheet
        Take-Home Activity: Is Your Mama a Llama?
        Llama Activity Sheet
        Recommended Books

Behavior 4   Elaborating on Ideas 131
        Class Activity: Extending a Story
        Take-Home Activity: Paper Bag Puppet
        Recommended Books

Afterword 135
References 137

Appendix A   Statistical Support for the ACIRI 143
Appendix B   Family Literacy Programs Case Study 155
                    with Amy Oak
Appendix C   Helpful Books and Web Sites 163

Contents of the CD-ROM

Welcome to *Let's Read Together: Improving Literacy Outcomes with the Adult–Child Interactive Reading Inventory (ACIRI)* CD-ROM
About the Author
About the Contributor
About This CD-ROM
About the Adult–Child Interactive Reading Inventory (ACIRI)

Adult–Child Interactive Reading Inventory (ACIRI)

English ACIRI Tool and Scoring Sheet
Spanish ACIRI Tool and Scoring Sheet

English Activities and Activity Sheets

Category I   Enhancing Attention to Text
with Adam Severson

        Behavior 1   Maintaining Physical Proximity
            Class Activity: Read Aloud
            "Where Did You Read with Your Child This Week?" Activity Sheet
            Take-Home Activity: Trust Walk

        Behavior 2   Sustaining Interest and Attention
            Class Activity: Telling a Story Together
            Take-Home Activity: I Spy

        Behavior 3   Holding the Book and Turning Pages
            Class Activity: Mouse Hunt
            Take-Home Activity: Animals Wearing Clothing
            "Animals Should Definitely NOT Wear Clothing!" Activity Sheet

        Behavior 4   Displaying a Sense of Audience
            Class Activity: Tell Me a Story
            Take-Home Activity: Making a Family Book

Category II   Promoting Interactive Reading and Supporting Comprehension
               with Adam Severson

               Behavior 1   Posing and Soliciting Questions
                   Class Activity: Nine Magic Wishes
                   Take-Home Activity: Guess What?

               Behavior 2   Identifying and Understanding Pictures and Words
                   Class Activity: Alphabet Book
                   Take-Home Activity: Riddles

               Behavior 3   Relating Content to Personal Experiences
                   Class Activity: A Terrible, Horrible, No Good, Very Bad Day
                   Class Activity: I Like It When…
                   Take-Home Activity: How We Grow
                   "Memories from When I Was…" Activity Sheet
                   "How I Looked…" Activity Sheet
                   "Memories of What It Was Like to Be My Child's Age" Activity Sheet
                   "How I Looked at My Child's Age" Activity Sheet

               Behavior 4   Pausing to Answer Questions
                   Class Activity: Animal Poetry
                   "A Poem About an Animal" Activity Sheet
                   "A Poem About Me" Activity Sheet
                   "A Poem About My Family" Activity Sheet
                   "A Poem from My Imagination" Activity Sheet
                   Take-Home Activity: Mama, Do You Love Me?
                   "A Sunny Day: A Story Filled with Questions" Activity Sheet

Category III   Using Literacy Strategies
               with Adam Severson

               Behavior 1   Identifying Visual Cues
                   Class Activity: Rebus Poems
                   "Rebus Poem" Activity Sheet
                   Take-Home Activity: Using Repeated Words
                   "Repeated Words" Activity Sheet

               Behavior 2   Predicting What Happens Next
                   Class Activity: What Might Happen Next?
                   12 "What Do You Think Is Going to Happen?" Activity Sheets
                   Class Activity: Picture Walk Predictions
                   "Predicting the Story" Activity Sheet
                   Take-Home Activity: If You Give a Mouse a Cookie
                   "Baking Cookies with Your Child" Activity Sheet
                   Take-Home Activity: Can You Predict What Will Happen?
                   "If You Give Someone You Love a Hug…" Activity Sheet

               Behavior 3   Recalling Information
                   Class Activity: Story Map
                   "Story Map" Activity Sheet
                   Take-Home Activity: Is Your Mama a Llama?
                   Llama Activity Sheet

Behavior 4   Elaborating on Ideas
    Class Activity: Extending a Story
    Take-Home Activity: Paper Bag Puppet

Spanish Activities and Activity Sheets

Categoría I   Brindando Mayor Atención a los Textos
con Adam Severson

    Comportamiento 1   Manteniendo la Proximidad Física
        Actividad de Clase: Leer en Voz Alta
        Hoja de Actividad "¿Dónde Leyó con Su Hijo Esta Semana?"
        Actividad para Trabajar en Casa: Caminata de Confianza

    Comportamiento 2   Mantenimiento del Interés y la Atención
        Actividad de Clase: Contando Juntos un Cuento
        Actividad para Trabajar en Casa: Yo Espío

    Comportamiento 3   Compartiendo el Libro y Pasando las Páginas
        Actividad de Clase: Búsqueda de Ratones
        Actividad para Trabajar en Casa: Animales Con Ropa Puesta
        Hoja de Actividad "¡Los Animales Definitivamente No Deben Ponerse
            Ropa!"

    Comportamiento 4   Tomando en Cuenta la Presencia del Niño
        Actividad de Clase: Cuéntame Una Historia
        Actividad para Trabajar en Casa: Haciendo un Libro de Familia

Categoría II   Promoviendo la Lectura Interactiva y Alentando la Comprensión
con Adam Severson

    Comportamiento 1   Formulando y Haciendo Preguntas
        Actividad de Clase: ¡No, David!
        Actividad para Trabajar en Casa: Adivine Qué

    Comportamiento 2   Identificando y Enteniendo Dibujos y Palabras
        Actividad de Clase: Libro del Alfabeto
        Actividad para Trabajar en Casa: Acertijos

    Comportamiento 3   Relacionando el Contenido con las Experiencias
    Personales
        Actividad de Clase: Un Día Terrible, Horrible, Espantoso, Horroso
        Actividad de Clase: ¡Me Gusto Como Soy!
        Actividad para Trabajar en Casa: Cómo Crecemos
        Hoja de Actividad "Los Recuerdos de Hace..."
        Hoja de Actividad "Cómo Me Veía..."
        Hoja de Actividad "Cómo Me Veía Cuando Tenía la Edad de Mi Hijo"
        Hoja de Actividad "Los Recuerdos de Cómo Era Cuando Yo Tenía la
            Edad de Mi Hijo"

    Comportamiento 4   Haciendo Pausas Para Contestar Preguntas
        Actividad de Clase: Poesía Acerca de Animales
        Hoja de Actividad "Un Poema Acerca de un Animal"
        Hoja de Actividad "Un Poema Acerca de Mí"

Hoja de Actividad "Un Poema Acerca de Mi Familia"
Hoja de Actividad "Un Poema Proveniente de Mi Imaginación"
Actividad para Trabajar en Casa: ¿Me Quieres, Mamá?
Hoja de Actividad "Un Día Soleado: Una Historia Llena de Preguntas"

Categoría III   Usando Estrategias Culturales
                con Adam Severson
        Comportamiento 1   Identificando las Señales Visuales
                Actividad de Clase: Poemas de Figuras
                Hoja de Actividad "Un Poema de Figuras"
                Actividad para Trabajar en Casa: Usando Palabras Repetidas
                Hoja de Actividad "Palabras Repetidas"
        Comportamiento 2   Prediciendo Qué Pasará
                Actividad de Clase: ¿Qué Piensa Que Va a Pasar?
                12 Hoja de Actividad "¿Qué Piensa Que Va a Pasar?"
                Actividad de Clase: Prediciendo la Historia
                Hoja de Actividad "Prediciendo la Historia"
                Actividad para Trabajar en Casa: Si le Das Una Galleta a un Ratón
                Hoja de Actividad "Haciendo Galletas con Su Hijo"
                Actividad para Trabajar en Casa: ¿Puede Predecir Lo Que Pasará?
                Hoja de Actividad "Si Le Da a Alguien Que Ama..."
        Comportamiento 3   Recordando Información
                Actividad de Clase: Mapa del Cuento
                Hoja de Actividad "Mapa del Cuento"
                Actividad para Trabajar en Casa: ¿Tu Mamá es Una Llama?
                Hoja de Actividad Llama
        Comportamiento 4   Elaborando Ideas
                Actividad de Clase: Extendiendo la Historia
                Actividad para Trabajar en Casa: Títere de Bolsa de Papel

About the Author

Andrea DeBruin-Parecki, Ph.D., is nationally recognized for her work in the field of family literacy. In addition to creating the Adult–Child Interactive Reading Inventory (ACIRI) tool, she has designed programs and acted as a consultant across the country. She has developed the Early Literacy Skills Assessment, a comprehensive, reliable, and valid tool in the form of a children's storybook that measures phonological awareness, alphabetic principle, comprehension, and concepts about print. She has expertise in emergent literacy, literacy within at-risk and minority populations, the motivation of at-risk populations, and assessment. She was a Fulbright Senior Specialist in Guatemala. Her work related to literacy development in young children and families has been published and presented at national, regional, and state conferences. She currently is Director of the High/Scope Early Childhood Reading Institute in Ypsilanti, Michigan.

About the Contributors

Adam Severson has a bachelor of arts degree in elementary education and a master of arts degree in reading and language arts, both from the University of Northern Iowa. He worked with Dr. DeBruin-Parecki to develop and implement a family literacy program in Waterloo, Iowa. Currently, he is a sixth-grade reading teacher in Des Moines, Iowa.

Amy Oak has an associate of arts degree focused on early childhood education from Stephens College in Columbia, Missouri. Her bachelor of science degree in social science is from the University of Massachusetts Amherst University Without Walls, and her elementary teaching credential is from the Center for Open Teaching and Learning, both located in Berkeley, California. Her master of education degree in special education is from Northwest Missouri State University. She coordinates trainings given by Dr. DeBruin-Parecki for local early childhood educators and has developed several family literacy series in collaboration with Dr. DeBruin-Parecki and local early childhood educators. Currently, she is the early childhood and literacy consultant at the Muskegon Area Intermediate School District, a regional service agency in Muskegon, Michigan.

Foreword

Parents reading aloud to their children is assumed to be a prerequisite for success in school. As early as 1908, Huey revealed that "the secret of it all lies in the parents reading aloud and with their child" (p. 32). In *Becoming a Nation of Readers,* the authors stated that "parents play roles of inestimable importance in laying the foundations for learning to read" (Anderson, Hiebert, Scott, & Wilkinson, 1985, p. 57). Mahoney and Wilcox concluded,

> If a child comes from a reading family where books are a shared source of pleasure, he or she will have an understanding of the language of the literacy world and respond to the use of books in a classroom as a natural expansion of pleasant home experiences. (1985, p. ix)

What I found in my 1989 study titled "Supporting Lower SES Mothers' Attempts to Provide Scaffolding for Book Reading" is that book reading is a very simple teacher directive but a very complex and difficult task for some parents. I put forth the argument that to simply inform parents of the importance of reading to their children is not sufficient. Instead, we must go beyond *telling* to *showing* parents of lower socioeconomic status how to participate in parent–child book-reading interactions with their children and supporting their attempts to do so.

While researchers like me and others argued that parents reading to their children was important, an instrument to help us to scientifically measure the interactive reading concurrently between an adult and a child was sorely missing. Andrea DeBruin-Parecki's book is the only one that addresses this topic with breadth and depth. It is both a timely and a significant book because the tool that she has developed is the first instrument of its kind. I am confident that this tool will be one that we as literacy educators will widely use. If this tool had been available more than 15 years ago when I first published my *Parents as Partners in Reading* program (1993), I would have readily used it.

This book is a strong scaffold for anyone wanting to try, or get better at, measuring interactive reading concurrently between an adult and a child. What Andrea DeBruin-Parecki has done in this book is lower the diving board so that, for all of us, holding our nose and jumping into measuring interactive reading is a much safer bet. And, DeBruin-Parecki's book helps us to begin our journey of making visible the standards and methods of interactive reading—a goal that some would argue is the most important goal to ensure success in school.

Patricia A. Edwards, Ph.D.
Professor of Language and Literacy
Michigan State University

REFERENCES

Anderson, R.C., Hiebert, E., Scott, J.A., & Wilkinson, I.A.G. (1985). *Becoming a nation of readers: The report of the commission of reading.* Washington, DC: The National Institute of Education.

Edwards, P.A. (1989). Supporting lower SES mothers' attempts to provide scaffolding for book reading. In J. Allen & J. Mason (Eds.), *Risk makers, risk takers, risk breakers: Reducing the risks for young literacy learners* (pp. 222–250). Portsmouth, NH: Heinemann.

Edwards, P.A. (1993). *Parents as partners in ready: A family literacy training program* (2nd ed.). Chicago: Childrens Press.

Huey, E.B. (1908). *The psychology and pedagogy of reading.* New York: MacMillan.

Mahoney, E., & Wilcox, L. (1985). *Ready, set, read: Best books to prepare preschools.* Metuchen, NJ: Scarecrow Press.

Acknowledgments

I have so many people to thank for the publication of this book. These are people who believe in me and have supported my work on the Adult–Child Interactive Reading Inventory (ACIRI) over the years. Without all of them, this book would not have been possible. I express my gratitude to them here.

Scott Paris was my dissertation chair and was there for me when the ACIRI was first imagined and has been ever since. His constant support and encouragement have enriched my life and made me a better person, scholar, and writer.

The teachers and staff at the Bendle/Carman-Ainsworth Learning Community in Flint, Michigan, especially Kristi Myatt, Judy Banfield, Violet Andersen, and Carolyn Ruttledge, were there when I needed a site to begin testing the ACIRI. They all helped me to make it a more effective instrument...*and* they are still using it!

Adam Severson, a former student and now a teacher and reading specialist, was at my side as I wrote the curriculum for the ACIRI. His collaboration made it far better.

Amy Oak and the folks at the Muskegon Area Intermediate School District, Michigan, were instrumental in piloting the instrument and activities with Hispanic populations.

Zong Ping Xiang generously gave of her time, helping with the statistics in Appendix A.

Heather Shrestha, Astrid Zuckerman, Amy Kopperude, and all of the folks at Brookes Publishing have been not only wonderful to work with but also patient beyond belief. I could never have found a greater group of people to help me through the publication process.

Finally, and most important, I want to thank my mother, who always read with me when I was young and instilled a love of books that to this day has only grown. I want to let my children, Larissa, Josh, and Emily, know that reading with them was always the highlight of my day. They have all grown to be adults now, and I know they one day will bring the magic of reading into their own children's lives. And to my HBMP, thank you for the constant support and encouragement.

Let's Read Together

Assessment of Interactive Reading

CHAPTER 1

Family Literacy and Interactive Reading

Throughout history, family literacy has consistently been present in homes and communities and across generations. Adults have always schooled children in some manner to assist them in becoming literate in the ways and traditions of their cultures. De Castell and Luke saw being literate as "having mastery over the processes by means of which culturally significant information is coded" (1983, p. 373). This information can be passed on in a variety of ways such as speaking, drawing, signing, gesturing, and singing, as well as through written text. The definition of literacy encompasses much more than conventional types of skills such as reading and writing. A person considered literate in one culture may be considered illiterate when judged by the standards of another.

As societies have been established throughout time, unique forms of literate communication are created and taught in family group settings. Prehistoric families symbolized information through shared cave drawings. Most likely, they discussed these paintings, asking questions, retelling the depictions, and perhaps predicting what might happen next. Scribes of the Greek and Roman culture, as well as those of the Middle Ages, were most often taught their skills by their fathers and close relatives. These scribes were men who could read and write, so their skills often led to discussion of the written text. Native American families passed their knowledge down through intricate storytelling, songs, and drawings.

A unique and well-documented example of family literacy and interactive reading practices in action can be seen in the diaries and journals of Cotton Mather, a preacher who lived between the late 17th and early 18th century in the Massachusetts Bay Colony. He fathered 16 children and had three wives in his lifetime (Monaghan, 1991). He felt it was his responsibility to teach his children and wives how to become literate in their society by learning to write and read. He also taught some of his slaves to read and write, an unusual activity in those times. Literacy was a communal activity that fostered interaction between his family members. He wrote his own books to use in their education. He felt strongly that a parent should be his or her children's first teacher. He espoused his philosophy by modeling skills; interpreting texts for and with children, using one text to expand, explain, or confirm another; assigning specific tasks; actively teaching by constructing bridges between life, language, and literacy; teaching strategy use; and using writing in the service of personal development (Monaghan, 1991). Cotton Mather intuitively knew the value of interactive reading.

Becoming literate in the ways of one's society seems to have always been politically charged. "The advance of literacy was increasingly accompanied by a lowered status and greater isolation of the illiterate, and by some devaluing of experience" (Clifford, 1984, p. 473). Those who possessed advanced knowledge began to separate themselves from those who did not, thus creating the literate/illiterate dichotomy. Women and the lower-class segments of populations were intentionally kept from learning more than they needed to know to "keep them in their place," thus ensuring the more menial and traditional roles they played in society. Conventional literacy acquisition was tied to context. Sanctioned teaching of people in lower classes and women occurred based on what they needed to be able to do in order to perform their jobs or to prepare their children to go on to the "real learning." Although many of these people were considered to be unschooled and conventionally illiterate according to societal norms established by a ruling class, they still were literate in the ways of their own cultural groups. This type of personal literacy did not, however, get them very far in the larger society. In order to advance their context-specific literacy skills to more general literacy skills, many families began to learn among themselves. Written texts were prized and difficult to get. As soon as people were able to get books and papers, they began to communicate around written text, and interactive reading skills came into practice.

Many groups of people over time have struggled to learn mainstream skills associated with power and position in a society. They have also struggled just because they want to know. Black slaves brought to this country in the 18th and 19th centuries attempted to learn to read and write with the knowledge that great personal harm could come to them if their owners found out. Slave narratives clearly depict the tremendous hardship suffered by those who learned to read and write and who taught others including family members late at night or during times they were unobserved (Genovese, 1974; Yetman, 1970). Between 1936 and 1939, ex-slaves told interviewers of their experiences with reading and writing.

> De white folks didn't allow us to even look at a book. Dey would scold and sometimes whip us iffen dey caught us with our head in a book. Dat is one thing I surely did want to do, and dat was to learn to read and write. (Mary Ella Grandberry, p. 145, as cited in Yetman, 1970)

> None of us have any learnin', weren't never allowed to pick up as much as a piece of paper. My daddy slip and get a Webster book and den he take it out in de field and he learn to read. De white folks afraid to let the chillen learn anythin'. They afraid dey get too smart and be harder to manage. Dey never let 'em know anythin' about anythin'. (Fannie Moore, p. 229, as cited in Yetman, 1970)

Slave narratives indicate that slaves who learned to read and write and who understood the depths of degradation and ignorance they experienced were eager to teach others most often through interactive reading and direct instruction so they could be more well-informed, regardless of personal risk. *Nightjohn,* a powerful children's novel by Gary Paulsen (1993), clearly depicts this motivation and the great chances slaves took to learn and teach others, as well as the horrible consequences of being caught. When slavery was abolished, many African Americans attended schools and came home to teach what they learned to other family members.

These few examples clearly show that family literacy and interactive reading is not a new concept. Perhaps family literacy was not formally defined or named prior to the 20th century, but it has always existed. If one considers family literacy to be members of immediate and extended family educating one another in diverse areas of knowledge through a variety of means, then family literacy has existed throughout history. It has occurred with and without the experience and modeling of formal schooling.

PROMOTING INTERACTIVE READING

Family literacy gained federal support in 1989 when Even Start was authorized as Title I, Chapter 1, Part B, of the Elementary and Secondary Education Act (ESEA) of 1965 (PL 89-10). In 2000, Even Start was renamed the William F. Goodling Even Start Family Literacy Program as Title I, Part B, Subpart 3, of ESEA. Even Start is a federally funded program that fights poverty by improving academic achievement of children and their families, particularly in the area of reading. This program provides educational services for the family so that children have the chance to experience high quality early education and parents/guardians are able to support children's development. Congressman William Goodling, who sponsored the legislation, characterized Even Start as a program that "supplies parents with the training to be their child's first teacher; allows them to gain needed literacy skills and to complete their formal education; and provides a preschool program for children" (1994, p. 24). St. Pierre and Swartz described Even Start as a family-focused program with the following three interrelated goals:

- to help parents become full partners in the education of their children

- to assist children in reaching their full potential as learners; and

- to provide literacy training for their parents. (1995, pp. 38–39)

The general philosophy of Even Start is connected to three of the eight National Education Goals that were achieved by the year 2000 first developed by President George H.W. Bush and the nation's governors in 1990 and elaborated in 1994 in the Goals 2000: Educate America Act (PL 103-227):

- Goal 1: All children in America will start school ready to learn.

- Goal 6: Every adult American will be literate and will possess the knowledge and skills necessary to compete in a global economy and exercise the rights and responsibilities of citizenship.

- Goal 8: Every school will promote partnerships that will increase parental involvement and participation in promoting the social, emotional, and academic growth of children.

These goals provide guidance in establishing program frameworks that promote adult literacy, teach parents to support the educational growth of their children, and prepare children for success in regular school programs. Meeting these goals will accomplish Even Start's overriding purpose to promote the parent as the child's first teacher.

Federal legislation—ESEA, Title I, Part B, Subpart 3—requires Even Start programs to make available the following four core components:

1. An early childhood education program for children from birth to age 8

2. An adult education program that helps adults develop basic educational and literacy skills, including basic or secondary adult education, English as a second language, or preparation for a General Education Development (GED) certificate

3. A parent education program to enhance parent–child interactions and parents' support of their children's growth and development

4. Interactive literacy activities between parents and their children

Even Start uses all four services to affect lasting change and improve children's achievement in school. Families must participate in each of the four components. Despite these mandates, local grantees still have significant flexibility in designing programs to best address their own community needs. The teaching of interactive reading skills is a key component of the majority of programs.

The following two anecdotes provide the reader with a more modern look at family literacy with a clear focus on interactive reading. These stories are from an Even Start program and emphasize what both individual and interactive learning means to parents and teachers. The 27-year-old mother of a 6-year-old boy and a 2-year-old girl had this to say:

> *Even Start means fun for me and my kids, and we learn new things. I'm working on my GED for myself, but I'm also learning new and fun things to do for my children and myself. My kids are so proud that they are learning new games; spending time with each other; saying their ABCs, 123s, and colors; and reading books together. Last but not least, I am learning things to teach my children so they will be smart, so they could also put their mind on something and grow.*

An experienced Even Start teacher, when asked about the Adult–Child Interactive Reading Inventory (ACIRI), stated:

> *I use interactive literacy in my Even Start home visits. One of the favorite activities of both parent and child is reading a book together. We often follow with an extension activity in a child- and parent-created book. For example, after Mom and Brandon read Eric Carle's* Dream Snow, *they created their own page in Brandon's journal. He drew a picture of his cat, Mittens, and blanketed him in snow with Wite-Out. A sentence dictated to Mom was written on the page. Brandon loves rereading this book he made with Mom.*

VALUE OF INTERACTIVE READING

The value of interactive reading has not changed over time. When interactive reading is practiced using skills that promote learning, it can be instrumental in promoting the development of the reading skills and motivational factors needed to become an effective reader. Interactive reading can be defined as reading aloud that includes conversation, relies on the give and take of turn taking, and involves children in the process (DeBruin-Parecki, 2004). Interactive reading serves multiple important purposes such as

- Prompting children's active involvement in constructing an understanding of a book's meaning by making inferences, drawing conclusions, and making predictions
- Clarifying children's understandings of a book
- Expanding children's understandings of vocabulary words
- Prompting children to use new vocabulary from a book in conversations about the book and in life
- Familiarizing children with concepts about print
- Helping children to become more aware of and attend to a variety of sounds including rhymes
- Providing opportunities for letter and sound identification
- Motivating children to gain a love for books and a desire to read

Interactive reading occurs in a range of settings and is carried out by a diverse cast of readers. One can see interactive reading between parents/guardians and their children, grandmothers/grandfathers and their grandchildren, and teachers and their students from preschool through their school years; in family literacy programs; and in places too numerous to mention in a list. Interactive reading can be engaging and instructional and just plain fun. *However,* if interactive reading is used for instructional purposes, particularly for developing effective prereading and reading skills, it is important to remember that *how* you read is key.

IMPORTANCE OF SUPPORTING INTERACTIVE READING

Although improving interactive reading skills is certainly not the only practice that will make a difference in children's school success, it is a major one. The incorporation and practice of specific behaviors during joint book reading has been shown to promote future academic success for children as they enter school (Cochran-Smith, 1984; Flood, 1977; Jordan, Snow, & Porche, 2000; Morrow, 1983; Paratore, 2003; Senechal, Cornell, & Broda, 1995). Children who are read to frequently (Scarborough & Dobrich, 1994) and whose parents, guardians, or caregivers demonstrate emotion and excitement in their reading (Sonnenschein & Munsterman, 2002) and particular strategies that encourage interaction while reading (DeBruin-Parecki, 2003; Martin & Reutzel, 1999; Whitehurst et al., 1988) tend to enter school more prepared to learn to read.

HOW POSITIVE INTERACTIVE READING EXPERIENCES AFFECT CHILD OUTCOMES

Over the years, popular media and academic research both have drawn attention to the benefits of reading to young children. Public service announcements on television encourage parents to read to their children. Stars such as Jamie Lee Curtis and LeVar Burton speak about reading to children in a variety of contexts. *Sesame Street, Between the Lions,* and *Reading Rainbow* on public television extol the virtues of interactive reading. Our president has often been seen reading with children. Many slogans similar to "Take children to new worlds, open up a book" pop up in a variety of places. Athletes visit schools to read with children. A multitude of organizations collect books at athletic events, bookstores, and other venues to give to children and their parents who have no books. And the list goes on.

The International Reading Association (IRA) and the National Association for the Education of Young Children (NAEYC) issued a joint position statement on learning to read and write (IRA/NAEYC, 1998) and have supported this idea. The release of the National Research Council Report *Preventing Reading Difficulties in Young Children* also confirms the widespread support of this notion (Snow, Burns, & Griffin, 1998).

Across the United States, there are a large variety of family literacy programs, federally funded programs such as Even Start, library programs, privately funded programs, school-based programs, and more. Programs have many goals, including providing social services, health and nutrition information, and excellent educational child care and/or schooling. Even with all of the differences in these programs, the one thread that ties them all together is interactive reading.

Over the years, researchers have found that interactive book reading enhances language development (Crain-Thoreson, Dahlin, & Powell, 2001; Dickinson & Tabors, 2001; Durkin, 1966, 1972; Storch & Whitehurst, 2001; Teale, 1978, 1981) and helps children learn that printed words, although different from oral language, represent sounds and carry meaning (Clay, 1979). A variety of studies have shown that early readers come from homes where adults read to them regularly and where books and reading materials are readily available (Bus, van IJzendoorn, & Pellegrini, 1995; Clark, 1976, 1984; Lancy, Draper, & Boyce, 1989; Morrow, 1983; Neuman, 1999; Purcell-Gates, 2000; Teale, 1978). Although specific joint storybook-reading behaviors and practices appear to enhance children's reading skills and comprehension, questions still remain about the specific characteristics of these interactive sessions that lead to children's success in reading. All of this research is discussed in more detail later in the chapter.

IDENTIFYING AND UNDERSTANDING INTERACTIVE READING BEHAVIORS

It is primarily through interactive dialogue that children gain comprehension skills, increase their understanding of literacy conventions, and are encouraged to enjoy reading. When adults and children are actively engaged in reading together as partners, they both naturally ask questions and make comments that assist the child in gaining understanding about the book's content, how books work, and what certain words and pictures represent. Book-reading episodes provide an opportunity for adults and children to co-construct knowledge in a social setting and negotiate meanings together. For example, if a child and adult are reading a book about dreaming, they can discuss their own dreams and how those relate to the dreams of the character in the book.

"Mothers must continually observe and reflect upon their children's interactions during book reading, interpret these interactions, and make decisions about the types of book reading strategies that will guide their children's understanding" (Martin & Reutzel, 1999, p. 1). Thus, the adult must be able to judge the child's current level of knowledge and know how to push the child a bit beyond that. Vygotsky (1978) called this working within the child's zone of proximal development. His theory claims that intellectual skills arise from social interactions that occur during practical activities. For instance, if an adult is reading a book that has a picture of cloudy skies, a question might be asked of the child regarding what might happen when the skies are cloudy. If the child says it could get cold, the adult might agree and then push the child a bit by remarking that cloudy skies often result in something else, something that can make puddles. At that point, the child might respond that cloudy skies can indicate rain.

In the context of literacy learning, Teale (1981) interpreted this to mean that, over time, children can internalize co-constructed parent-supported behaviors and strategies used during joint book-reading sessions. This, Teale argued, can eventually lead to independent functioning and self-regulated reading behaviors. For example, if an adult consistently asks a child prediction questions each time they read together, the child is more likely to begin asking them of him- or herself and of the adult. So, it might not be unusual for this child to say when reading with the adult, "I wonder what this story is about" or "I wonder what will happen next in the story." Furthermore, if the adult demonstrates strategies such as using pictures to determine what might happen, then the child most likely will begin to do the same.

Whitehurst and colleagues (1988) studied a method called *dialogic reading*, a way of reading picture books with children that differs from the typical way books are shared. The interaction that takes place requires a shift in roles in which the parent/guardian becomes an active listener who asks questions, adds information, and prompts the child to elaborate on ideas. Open-ended questions, rather than questions that ask just for a yes or no response are an important part of dialogic reading. Dialogic reading enhances children's expressive vocabulary and the grammatical complexity of children's speech when children are read to individually or in small groups. The interaction between the adult and child is the key. Thus, it is clear that reading one to one with a young child using dialogic reading will produce the best results.

In 1990, Morrow identified nine interactive reading behaviors that researchers have continued to investigate as leading to positive outcomes for young children's future success in reading. These behaviors include

1. Questioning

2. Scaffolding dialogue and responses

3. Offering praise or positive reinforcement

4. Giving or extending information

5. Clarifying information

6. Restating information

7. Directing discussion

8. Sharing personal reactions

9. Relating concepts to life experiences

As these behaviors have been examined, they also have been elaborated to make them clearer to practitioners and parents (DeBruin-Parecki, 1999, 2003). In addition to practicing these behaviors during interactive reading sessions, it also is important for adults to promote positive attitudes toward reading through enthusiasm, animation, and modeling (Bergin, 2001; Hiebert, 1981; Holdaway, 1979). For instance, the child who reads with an adult who gives the characters different voices, sounds excited about the story, and demonstrates a love of reading has a very different experience from the child who reads with an adult who has a monotone voice, cannot wait to finish the story, and clearly does not enjoy reading with the child or reading alone. An important emotional and physical connection takes place during interactive reading. "The rhythm of a mother's voice and the warmth of her touch invites young children to participate in the book reading event" (Martin, 1998, p. 1). Reading sessions also provide a natural context for adults to assist children in forming concepts about books, print, and reading, such as directionality and book handling (Clay, 1979). While getting ready to read and actually reading, adults can explain to children about the parts of a book, the function of the author and illustrator, how print goes from left to right, and more.

A number of studies have indicated that specific types of interactive reading behaviors are instrumental in developing successful reading habits for children. These studies all use different methods to demonstrate their findings. Many of them dwell on the differences between various cultures and socioeconomic status (SES) in regard to the frequency and quality of interactive reading sessions between adults and children. Most suggest that behaviors such as mutual questioning and responding, making stories relevant to the child's life, giving praise and feedback, explaining, physically sharing the book, monitoring a child's understanding, and adjusting dialogue to acknowledge mutual understanding all are behaviors that enhance children's literacy skills and comprehension (Cochran-Smith, 1984, 1986; Flood, 1977; Jordan et al., 2000; Ninio & Bruner, 1978; Roser & Martinez, 1985; Whitehurst et al., 1988).

If conversation takes place around the story as adults and young children read together, they are able to construct meaning together and build joint understandings. As demonstrated earlier in the chapter, the conversation must contain specific behaviors such as questioning, predicting, summarizing or retelling, connecting to real life, having the child in close proximity, and more. The following studies explain the value of using these behaviors while reading with a child.

RESEARCH SUPPORTING SPECIFIC
INTERACTIVE READING BEHAVIORS

Ninio and Bruner (1978) did a case study of a mother and her young child over a period of 10 months. They observed the mother reading picture books to her son, and they found a distinct pattern that occurred during these readings. The mother and child took part in a routine interactive dialogue in which the child labeled items in the book's pictures. This dialogue was identified as having four steps:

1. Attention-getting dialogue

2. Questioning

3. Labeling

4. Feedback

This case study showed a give-and-take routine between mother and child as they spoke to one another focused on the book's contents. As the child grew, the mother was able to judge when to assist him and when his understanding was complete enough to participate on his own. Her feedback became a scaffold allowing the child to learn eventually to do these things on his own. At the start, the mother could have asked the child, "What's that?" This would allow the child to identify objects in a book. If the child got them wrong, the mother could have provided gentle feedback to correct him. As the child got older, the mother might have asked, "What's that?" If the child did not know, the mother might have provided hints that related the object to something the child knew to help him identify the object.

Ninio and Bruner (1978) provided an early glimpse of what occurs during interactive reading sessions with very young children and the positive outcomes that can result. Although a lot can be learned from this study, it is limited in that its subject area is narrow: one male child from a middle-class Caucasian family.

Cochran-Smith (1984, 1986) studied storybook reading between adults and preschool children using observation, interviewing, and audiotaping of story readings over a period of 18 months. Those participating in this study were middle class and identified themselves as being school oriented with beliefs in the importance of strong literacy skills for lifetime academic and intellectual success. Cochran-Smith (1986) found obvious turn-taking patterns in which adults and children exchanged questions and answers, which enriched the child's understanding of the text as well as of the conventions of print and language. She also discovered that conversations that promoted the most interest and response were those that involved the connection of real life to text. Children appeared to be eager to accommodate new information into their existing schemas. For example, if a child had never seen snow but had seen rain, an adult might be able to assist the child in understanding the concept of snow using the concept of rain he or she already understood. Cochran-Smith stated, "The task of becoming literate and learning to make sense of printed and pictorial texts requires more than simply breaking the sound-symbol code" (1986, p. 39). Equally important is negotiation of meaning and understanding of literacy conventions that clearly can occur through interactive reading sessions.

Flood (1977) investigated the relationship between parental style of reading to young children and the child's performance on prereading-related tasks. The study consisted of tape recording 36 $3^1/_2$– to $4^1/_2$-year-old children and adults reading together in their homes. The sample was balanced for ethnicity and SES. The recordings were analyzed to determine characteristics that predict reading success for children. Flood found that the best predictors of success on the tasks were the number of questions answered by the child, number of words spoken by the child, number of warm-up preparatory questions asked by the parent, number of questions asked by the child, postevaluative questions, and positive reinforcement by the adults. As a result of this, he claimed that interactive reading between adults and children can be viewed as a cycle involving the following four steps, which are reflected in the behaviors assessed on the ACIRI, to produce effective results:

1. Children profit from preparation for reading with warm-up questions.

2. Children need to be part of the process (e.g., asking questions, relating content to present and past experiences).

3. Parents need to reinforce children's efforts.

4. Postevaluative questions complete the cycle and help children learn to assess, evaluate, and integrate.

Roser and Martinez (1985) analyzed the story language of four parents reading to their 3- to 4-year-old children in their homes in an attempt to gain insight on the individual role of the adult during joint storybook reading. They concluded that an adult tends to serve as

- A co-responder, by describing, reviewing, sharing personal reactions, and inviting child responses

- An informer-monitor, by explaining information about literacy conventions, explaining parts of the story, and assessing and monitoring the child's understanding

- A director, by introducing the story, announcing the conclusion, and managing the discussion

Each of these roles provides opportunities for modeling and scaffolding. Roser and Martinez found that the more children participate in these types of discussions, the more likely they are to take on some of these adult roles. The authors stated, "The value of an adult partner who shares books and who thinks aloud in response to literature cannot be ignored" (1985, p. 489).

Whitehurst et al. (1988) assessed a 1-month home-based intervention that was designed to promote optimal interactive reading between parents and children. The experimental group was asked to increase their use of open-ended questions and to respond more frequently to children's questions and expand on them. They were also asked to decrease straight reading of text. The control group was told to read as they usually did. The children were 21–35 months of age, and all were from two-parent, middle-class homes. The study found that children in the experimental group did significantly better on tests of expressive language ability. A follow-up 9 months later showed that this increase held, although the significance of the difference was not as great. The authors do not claim that the intervention is the only reason for this increase, as children develop language for a variety of reasons under a variety of circumstances. They only offer this as one variable that may enhance the process.

Kindergarten and first-grade children and their parents in an ethnically mixed, middle/working-class community participated in a study by Lancy and Draper (1988, as cited in Lancy et al., 1989) that examined the range of interaction patterns occurring during joint storybook reading. Through the analysis of videotapes and audiotapes, the researchers determined parents could be classified as using two different strategies: expansionist and reductionist. The expansionists emphasized partnership and responded to children's inquiries, asked questions, physically shared the book with their children, and generally involved children in the process of reading. The reductionists saw reading time as a test and forced children to perform and concentrate on decoding and error correction. The study found that children whose parents were expansionists enjoyed reading and were eager to learn. The children of reductionists tended to try to get through books as quickly as possible and did not find reading a pleasurable experience. The researchers concluded that those children who enjoy books and reading are more likely to become better readers, and parents can certainly assist them in developing this attitude by making joint reading an enjoyable learning experience.

According to Wasik and Bond (2001), interactive book reading can promote the development of language and literacy skills in young children. Their 15-week study was done in a Title I early learning center in Baltimore where more than 100 children from low SES families were placed in one of two groups: the interactive reading group, where teachers interactively read to the children and provided extension activities and materials related to the book, and the control group, which was not trained in interactive reading techniques and was provided nothing but books. Interactive reading techniques that were taught to the teachers in the first group consisted of previewing vocabulary, asking open-ended questions, and providing children with opportunities to talk and be heard. All of these behaviors make up the categories of the ACIRI. Results on standardized measures showed that the children in the interactive reading group performed better on vocabulary measures than those in the control group. So if adults read with children in ways that involve them and allow them opportunities to be partners in the process, they will gain vocabulary and understanding. For example, if an adult is reading the book *Frederick* by Leo Lionni, a story about a mouse who is a poet and does not join in the work of others, the child might be asked why he or she thinks Frederick does not work. As the child tries to explain, he or she uses multiple words and expresses his or her beginning understanding of the book. Later, when the child finds out that Frederick is a poet and has saved the words he has collected to brighten the cold winter of the others, he or she is exposed to more descriptive vocabulary. The adult can ask the child to use Frederick's words and others to describe a sunny day or try to make up a poem like Frederick does.

HOW INTERACTIVE READING
BEHAVIORS HELP CHILDREN LEARN

The studies presented previously support the notion that certain types of behaviors practiced during joint storybook reading time between adults and children result in children becoming more engaged in reading, achieving better comprehension of a story, increasing their vocabulary, and gaining an understanding of the conventions of books. In particular, mutual question asking and responding, making stories relevant to a child's life, praise and feedback, explanation, physically sharing a book, and monitoring a child's understanding and adjusting mutual dialogue to acknowledge this all are behaviors that appear to enhance children's literacy skills and understanding.

THE IMPACT OF CULTURAL,
ECONOMIC, AND ENVIRONMENTAL
DIFFERENCES ON INTERACTIVE READING SKILLS

Diverse cultures, economic backgrounds, and environments have a clear impact on the development of interactive reading skills. Teale (1978, 1981, 1984) has extensively reviewed the literature on early reading. He stated that although storybook reading may not be necessary for becoming literate, it does have an extremely facilitative effect on children's acquisition of emergent literacy skills. Students who come from disadvantaged environments with few books in their homes and few opportunities to read with adults may do fine in school. However, "The more conducive to learning to read we can make that environment, the more responsible it will be in the long run for enabling children to read and for fostering within children the desire to read" (1978, p. 931).

Within her larger ethnographic study of language use and communication in the Caucasian working-class community of Roadville, the African American working-class farm community of Trackton, and the mainstream community of Maintown in families that were typically middle class and Caucasian, Heath (1983, 1986) looked specifically at storybook reading. She discovered that Trackton parents did not read to their children, whereas Roadville and Maintown parents did. Maintown parents mediated the text for their children, taught them to label things and pay attention to specific aspects of the text, and demonstrated how to link old and new knowledge and to give "what" explanations (i.e., known-answer questions such as "What is that?" while pointing to a ball). Children learned to answer decontextualized knowledge questions and become cooperative conversation partners with adults in negotiating meaning from books. Roadville children were taught alphabet letters, words, and labeling but little generalization to other contexts. They were expected to listen and not interrupt and to focus on the truth in stories. Use of imagination was not considered desirable. Direct instruction was practiced as books were read to children; children were rarely asked to relate the book content to other areas. When Maintown children entered school, they usually did quite well, and this continued throughout elementary school. Roadville children appeared to do well when they first entered school because they understood adherence to rules and norms of participation. It was when the children entered the third or fourth grade and were expected to think more creatively and conceptually that they began to fail. Trackton children came to school not understanding the need for "what" explanations and therefore rarely participated. They had a hard time adjusting to the social interactional patterns of school learning and frequently did not meet with academic success. Heath's work demonstrates that it is not joint book reading itself but what goes on during the reading time that may make a strong difference in children's literacy development.

Swift (1970) designed a project to assess the effectiveness of a training program for enhancing the storytelling and communication skills of low-income mothers with limited educational backgrounds. Swift focused on aspects of maternal language and communication that were shown to be related to children's future success in school. Mothers of 3- to 5-year-old children in a Get Set preschool program were taught to use children's books to increase interactive communication with their children. The elaboration of thoughts was emphasized, as was sharing the books themselves, relating the books to the children's lives and experiences, and retelling stories. Mothers also were shown techniques for observing their child's reactions and responding to them. As a result of this intervention, mothers developed the ability to tell stories and interact with their children around books and began to better understand their role as teacher to their children. Children also became more attentive and responsive. Swift concluded that if mothers who are known to lack these skills could be taught to use preschool books as vehicles for communicating with their children, then their own language and literacy development would be positively affected, as would the literacy development of their children.

Paratore, Melzi, and Krol-Sinclair (1999) explored the experiences of Latino children whose parents participated in an intergenerational literacy project. They found that second-language parents, meaning those parents whose first language was not English, were limited in their involvement with their children in interactive reading sessions due to their educational and skill levels. However, the parents' interest in helping their children was not related to either of these factors or shared literacy experiences in a variety of contexts other than books. In order for second-language parents to be supportive of their young children's literacy development, they need to be provided opportunities to learn from and collaborate with those who have the knowledge to assist the parents. Their children's teachers, family literacy teachers, and others can fill this role. Asking parents whose first language is other than English to read in English without the support of bilingual teachers who can assist them can lead to parents' feelings of incompetence and lack of motivation to continue (Vernon-Feagans, Hammer, Miccio, & Manlove, 2003).

After examining a number of studies that focus on families and literacy, Rebecca Rogers (2001) documented three important things to remember about the status of literacy in families and communities. First, a wide range of practices exist. Second, literacy is a social practice that shapes and is shaped by social institutions. Third, social debates concerning family literacy are often connected to a discussion of the mismatch between home, community, and school discourse. With this in mind, we must continue to be aware that being literate can mean different things in different cultures. Parents encourage literacy in a variety of ways within the home and community. It does appear, however, that certain literacy practices that occur within joint book-reading episodes as illustrated by the behaviors on the ACIRI can help to promote the type of skills children need to master in order to ensure success in school. Evidence shows that nonmainstream groups believe this to be true (Edwards, 2004; Heath, 1983; McCarthey, 2000).

Although all cultures pass on literacy behaviors to their children in one form or another, ethnically diverse populations need to understand that specific ways of interacting around books can have a positive impact on children's academic futures. The types of interactive behaviors discussed earlier in this chapter (e.g., questioning, making information relevant to children's lives, engaging children through animated voices and excitement, having children close while reading) can be taught to parents in different cultural contexts, in different languages, and using culturally relevant texts, and parents can be encouraged to practice them during storybook reading and oral storytelling with their children.

PARADIGMS FOR MEASURING ADULT–CHILD BEHAVIORS DURING JOINT READING SESSIONS

Before the ACIRI, no tool was available to measure interactive reading concurrently between an adult and a child. Attempts to measure interactive reading have focused on either the adult or the child. Although understanding the literacy skill levels of adults and children separately is important, this tells little about how they read together. If the interaction between the adult and the child promotes greater understanding and skill development, particularly for the child in most cases, documenting what goes on during this process is important. If a teacher knows what an adult and child are doing together during storybook reading sessions, assisting them in developing more effective practices leading to advanced development of important skills is a far easier task. Because no tools other than the ACIRI are available to accomplish this, the following section explores two interactive reading instruments that exist that look at *only* the adult or the child.

Parent as Reader Scale

Guinagh and Jester (1972) developed the Parent as Reader Scale (PARS) to assess the quality of the mother–child interaction during reading and to determine the quality of the mother's teaching ability. The focus was on the mother's behaviors. The items on the scale were selected to reflect those dimensions of the mother–child interaction that were assumed to be related to positive growth in the child. The PARS items cover introduction to book, language use, encouragement of child participation, elaboration, feedback, identification, and affect. Ten different rating scales are assessed by scores ranging from 1 to 5. The highest total score possible is 50. This instrument was used with low-SES populations to determine which important reading and teaching behaviors parents may not currently use when reading with their children. Guinagh and Jester designed this tool as a springboard for training parents to read more effectively during storybook time.

Mothers Reading to Infants: An Observational Tool

Resnick and colleagues (1987) developed an evaluation tool for observing behaviors during maternal reading to infants. Their instrument comprises four categories: 1) mother's body management, 2) management of book, 3) language proficiency, and 4) attention to affect. A total of 56 separate behaviors are listed under these categories. Although the authors were familiar with theory on early reading, they chose to arrive at these behaviors by observing what occurred during mother–infant reading sessions as seen on videotape. They felt that they wanted to be open to all aspects of sharing behavior and did not want to narrow their instrument based on others' findings. The instrument does ultimately include many of the well-researched behaviors such as labeling, praise, description, affect, identification, making text relevant to life, and inviting participation. However, a stronger emphasis is on physical behaviors such as holding the child close, removing distractions, and sharing the book rather than on behaviors that directly develop skills such as predicting and identifying. When the mothers are scored, both positive and negative behaviors are considered.

In their initial study, Resnick and colleagues (1987) found that mothers became more involved as their children grew older and were able to express their understanding and participate frequently. This is supported by Martin (1998), who found that as children get older they can be provided with more factual information about book concepts by their mothers and that more demands are placed on the children to label and participate in dialogue. Resnick and colleagues believe that use of their instrument is helpful in identifying those adults who may benefit most from some type of training in positive reading behaviors. By helping parents practice reading behaviors that have been shown to enhance the reading readiness of children when they enter school, children who might have previously met with frustration may now find success. Most notably, Edwards (1991, 1995) has used Resnick and colleagues' observation instrument to assist in determining the types of behaviors parents are taught in her training program, Parents as Partners in Reading.

Few attempts have been made to construct instruments that assess the interactive reading behaviors of parents and their preschool children, particularly in the home environment. Some studies have examined interactive behaviors between teachers and students in schools using self-designed rating scales (Klesius & Griffith, 1996; Morrow, 1990), but these scales have not been promoted as evaluation tools for parents and children.

The two instruments presented previously focus exclusively on rating adult behavior but not on the corresponding behaviors of the child. If the quality of interaction between adult and child promotes literacy development, then it is important to evaluate the behaviors of both participants in order to determine instructional strategies that may assist them.

SOLVING THE DILEMMA OF INTERACTIVE READING MEASUREMENT

In order to effectively measure interactive reading behaviors, professionals need a tool that has a dual focus on the adult and the child. Chapter 2 introduces the reader to the Adult–Child Interactive Reading Inventory (ACIRI), a tool that measures the behaviors of an adult and a child at the same time as they read interactively. It can be used not only as an evaluation instrument but also as a guide for individualized instruction and learning (DeBruin-Parecki, 1999, 2003).

Understanding the Adult–Child Interactive Reading Inventory

Why is the Adult–Child Interactive Reading Inventory (ACIRI) important?

> Children are not born knowing how to connect their knowledge and experience in 'literate' ways to printed and pictorial texts. Rather, they must learn strategies for understanding texts just as they must learn the ways of eating and talking that are appropriate to their cultures or social groups. (Cochran-Smith, 1986, p. 36)

For children to develop effective early literacy skills and habits that lead to increased comprehension, improved critical thinking, consistent use of strategies, and motivation to learn, parents need to play a major part. After all, parents are their children's first teachers. Parents teach their children from the time they are born. Parents talk to children so they learn to listen and recognize and use language. Parents help their children learn to walk, tie their shoes, and do innumerable other things. They often are unaware of the powerful teaching role they play in their young children's lives. This includes teaching early literacy skills. Valuable instruction in early literacy skills can take place naturally within multiple contexts such as shopping at the grocery store, riding in the car, eating in a restaurant, and cooking together. New vocabulary is abundant in different situations, and children learn to listen and understand. One special context for valuable instruction is during enjoyable interactive reading sessions between parent and child. When a parent and a child read together, they can form a close emotional bond in addition to the literacy skills learned. When an adult and child sit close together and read a story, they will more likely be involved in the plot together. This encourages a child's natural curiosity, and with skilled assistance from the adult partner, the child can develop all-important skills such as retelling, letter identification, and rhyming.

As mentioned in Chapter 1, the incorporation and practice of specific behaviors during joint storybook reading have been shown to promote future academic success for children as they enter school (Cochran-Smith, 1984; Flood, 1977; Jordan et al., 2000; Morrow, 1983; Senechel, Cornell, & Broda, 1995). Remember, it is not only *that* adults read to children but also and more important *how* adults read to children that make a difference in their development of literacy skills important to future success in school. Although improving interactive reading skills is certainly not the only goal of family literacy and preschool programs, it is a major one. The desire to help their children learn to read so they will become academically successful is one of the primary reasons adults choose to attend family literacy programs and workshops (Brizius & Foster, 1993; Cairney, 2000; Edwards, 1995).

If a person were to walk into most family literacy or preschool programs in communities or schools almost anywhere in the United States today and ask to see evidence of improved adult–child joint book-reading practices, staff would unlikely be able to provide this information in a systematic manner (DeBruin-Parecki, Paris, & Seidenberg, 1997). Standardized tests, which are most commonly used to provide information on the progress of participants, are not useful for this purpose as they are designed to separately measure adult and child development of reading skills and cannot indicate any form of interactive growth. Standardized tests do not demonstrate how the adult has learned to provide more positive and interesting reading experiences for his or her children; neither do they measure how young children initiate or respond to conversation during joint book reading.

The ACIRI is designed to evaluate key interactive reading practices and to assist programs and families in measuring the progress being made as adults and children learn to read together. This tool offers teachers and participants information about interactive literacy behaviors that promote positive outcomes (DeBruin-Parecki, 2003). This book not only describes how to use the ACIRI but also offers useful discussions of the most important behaviors for professionals to recognize and support to promote positive interactive reading experiences between caregivers and children.

UNDERSTANDING THE ADULT–CHILD INTERACTIVE READING INVENTORY

The ACIRI is designed to be an observational interactive reading tool that is not patronizing, insulting, or threatening to parents, caregivers, or children. It is a tool that provides a means for family literacy teachers to assess joint storybook reading and to teach parents effective techniques for making reading more interesting and useful to their children. The ACIRI is used to observe adult–child dyads under natural conditions during joint storybook reading time in homes, in preschool centers, and in a variety of other settings. The tool consists of three categories of behaviors selected for inclusion based on research in the field of early literacy skill development.

PURPOSES OF THE ADULT–CHILD INTERACTIVE READING INVENTORY

The ACIRI tool in English and Spanish is an authentic, reliable, and valid assessment tool, teaching tool, and program design and evaluation tool. The inventory was primarily created to

- Provide teachers working with both parents and children a means of evaluating each dyad to assist the teacher in focusing future instruction to be effective for each adult and each child

- Enable parents to learn how they can improve in order to assist their child in developing the kinds of literacy skills that appear to be most helpful in ensuring success when children enter school

- Act as a pre- and postassessment to provide data for program evaluation purposes

- Provide guidelines for family literacy program design when the focus is on improving early literacy skills

- Train teachers and tutors to incorporate research-based behaviors during their interactive reading sessions with children

CONTENTS OF THE ADULT–CHILD INTERACTIVE READING INVENTORY

Three major categories divide the adult–child literacy behaviors. These categories are Enhancing Attention to Text, Promoting Interactive Reading and Supporting Comprehension, and Using Literacy Strategies. Each category contains four interactive behaviors for a total evaluation of 12 specific literacy behaviors for adults and 12 for children. These 12 behaviors are directly linked to the literature on promoting good reading practice (see Chapter 1 and Categories I, II, and III for specific information). Each of these behaviors is clearly defined in this chapter, and guidelines for observation are provided in Chapter 3.

Category I: Enhancing Attention to Text

Children must have role models in order to become readers. Whether these role models are parents, grandparents, brothers, sisters, or teachers, relationships must be formed. Children need to feel they can trust adults in their lives when learning to read. They draw near to others with whom they feel they have close relationships in the hopes that those people can provide them with things they feel are needed (Howe, Brandon, Hinings, & Schofield, 1999). The first four behaviors on the ACIRI involve enhancing children's attention to texts, and each of these behaviors reflects the need for a relationship to be established between adult and child.

"A central tenet of attachment theory is that there exists a 'shared dyadic program' in infants and caregivers, such that infant attachment behaviors elicit proximity-promoting behaviors in caregivers" (Bowlby, 1969, as cited in Nash & Hay, 2003, p. 222). Bowlby (1973) saw the establishment of a secure relationship between an adult and a child as a prerequisite for an effective collaborative context for activities such as joint book reading. In other words, when a child feels secure in the relationship with his or her parent or caregiver, he or she is much more likely to feel free to respond and interact with that person. If the child is insecure or afraid, he or she most likely will feel intimidated and thus unwilling to participate.

Maintaining Physical Proximity

The first behavior in Category I of the ACIRI is maintaining physical proximity. When the adult reads to the child, he or she needs to sit close to the child. That proximity is necessary to form and/or maintain the bond between the adult and child. It is crucial when reading with a child to make sure he or she is close to the adult caregiver so they can easily become shared partners in the reading. Attachment theory also helps to explain the second behavior on the ACIRI in this category.

Sustaining Interest and Attention

In order for a child to be engaged in the joint reading of a storybook, an adult must work to sustain the child's interest (e.g., smiling, acknowledging the child's comments, adjusting language, providing positive feedback). One example of sustaining a child's interest is changing voices for different characters in a story. According to Belsky and Cassidy (1994), children indicate that they are interested in interacting with adults in various ways. Smiling, talking, and laughing all are indications that children are enjoying interacting with adults. Adults need to be conscious of these indications when reading with children. "When parents and caregivers make reading enjoyable, they promote positive feelings about books and the purposes of reading" (Wolfe & Nevills, 2004, p. 56).

Holding the Book and Turning Pages

The key tenet of attachment theory is that attachment is shared between two people, typically a young child and a more mature caregiver (Nash & Hay, 2003). When reading with children, it is important to *let children hold the book and turn the pages,* the third behavior in Category I. The sharing of the book between adult and child fits right into the attachment model. When an adult and child are in a secure relationship, the adult acts as a positive model for the child. The adult demonstrates how to hold a book and turn pages while the child is comfortably engaged in interaction. The child is then more likely to do the same.

Displaying a Sense of Audience

To read with a child is a multifaceted task. One of the key parts of this task is for the adult to be able to share the book with the child by displaying a sense of audience when reading together. The adult needs to hold the book so the child can become part of the story, too. It is important that the child see the pages and pictures as the adult reads along. This allows for close interaction around a number of different behaviors such as pointing at pictures and words.

This encourages the child to initiate responses and interact with the adult as an engaged reading partner. Trevarthen and Aitken (2001) demonstrated that children are conscious and intentional with their interactions with other people. Adults need to be sure to share the book with children when reading with them so that children will become active participants.

Category II: Promoting Interactive Reading and Supporting Comprehension

Adults and children need to be interactive when reading in order to maximize the experience. This interactivity helps to promote and support reading comprehension. Since understanding what is being read is a primary goal, the behaviors in this category are of great importance.

Posing and Soliciting Questions

Effective questions have shown positive effects on children's comprehension and retention of information (Kertoy, 1994; Paris & Paris, 2003). Adults need to question children as they share books in order to be sure that the children understand the text. Children need to feel comfortable reading and have a sense of involvement in the reading process. Questioning children is crucial in helping them to feel a part of reading. It is also imperative that they are asked questions so they get a chance to talk about what is read (Armbruster, Lehr, & Osborn, 2003). Questions should go beyond the obvious ones that call for information and should ask "why" and "how" questions that make children think and demonstrate their comprehension of the story.

Identifying and Understanding Pictures and Words

Pointing to pictures and words, the second behavior in this category, helps children to identify and understand what is being read (Wolfe & Nevills, 2004). Since pictures and words are representations of ideas, people, and objects, pointing out pictures and words to children leads to greater understanding of the connection between representations and life and thought. Print awareness is part of the developmental process of reading (Clay, 1985). It is important that children distinguish the differences between print and other visual information (Adams, 1990). Books about numbers and the alphabet are ideal in practicing this behavior (Whitehead, 2002).

Relating Content to Personal Experiences

The third behavior in this category and another important aspect of interactive reading is relating the book's content and the child's responses to personal experiences. Talking about books and connections that children make to the content engages the children in the reading experience. Relating stories to personal experiences also deepens comprehension (Armbruster et al., 2003). Effective learners and readers feel part of the reading process when meaningful connections are made to the text (Billmeyer, 2003).

Pausing to Answer Questions

Pausing to answer the child's questions is the final behavior in this category. This requires the adult to listen to his or her child and to know where in the book might be a good time to try and solicit a question from the child. The adult must really practice taking time to make sure that children have the opportunity to ask questions. Feldman (2003) noted that wait time is critical in eliciting further thinking. It is very easy to read through a story without pausing so children have chances to speak on their own. Children also need to feel comfortable asking questions of adults. Allowing children the time to ask questions without adult prompting is very important in helping them gain understanding and to feel a part of the reading process.

Category III: Using Literacy Strategies

Literacy strategies are very important tools in teaching children to read and are particularly useful in promoting comprehension. For example, asking a child to recall information from the story indicates what the child remembers as well as what is important to him or her. This demonstrates what the child may understand about the story. The third category of behaviors on the ACIRI focuses on literacy strategies that parents may use as they read with their children. The need for utilizing these strategies is supported by a wide range of research. For example, Pearson, Roehler, Dole, and Duffy (1992) demonstrated that children learn to understand and love reading if they are engaged in what they read. The study showed that employing strategies such as using visual cues, making predictions, summarizing the story, and elaborating on the text all aid in comprehension. (For further research support of strategy use, see Chapter 1.)

Using Visual Cues

Using visual cues, the first behavior in Category III, assists in understanding text. Print awareness is knowing about print, books, and how they are used (Clay, 1979). Pictures help a young child understand a story. A child using pictures can easily demonstrate his or her comprehension skills as well as awareness of visual cues in the form of art or repetitive words (McGee & Richgels, 2003). Print awareness is visual and can help children understand what is going on in books (Armbruster et al., 2003). Young children also tend to be fond of picture books. Picture books are full of visual cues. Showing children cues they can see as they are following a story is an easy method of increasing their comprehension. When a child reads the book *Is Your Mama a Llama?* (Guarino, 2004), the title phrase is repeated throughout the book, allowing the child to chime in regularly and begin to recognize the words in print.

Asking Children to Predict What Is Going to Happen in the Story

The second behavior in this category, asking children to predict what happens next in the story, is an extremely important literacy strategy. Simply asking children, "What do you think will happen next?" can get them thinking about a story. Predictions also give adults insights as to how children are thinking as the pair shares a book. These predictions can let adults know if the children are understanding what is being read. Reading predictable books (e.g., *If You Give a Mouse a Cookie, Is Your Mama a Llama?*) also can get children to recognize repeated words and phrases (Armbruster et al., 2003). Making predictions gives children excellent opportunities to develop thinking skills as they read (Billmeyer, 2003).

Recalling Information from the Story

In order to know if children understand what they have read, checking to see what they can recall, the third behavior in this category, is valuable. Hansen (2004) stated that retelling can improve comprehension of a story. Oral retelling is a great strategy to use with children, especially when they cannot write. Having children draw pictures to retell a story is another way to assess how well they comprehend text. Regardless of how children show they can recall information, retelling a story can act as a great tool for improving comprehension (Paris & Paris, 2003).

Offering Ideas About the Story

Elaborating on a child's ideas about the story, the final behavior in this category, is necessary to foster a love of reading, deepen comprehension, and make children feel like reading partners. Parental behavior during reading has been proven to have an impact in forming a base for children as they become readers (Resnick et al., 1987). Children need to feel they can offer ideas about a story when they see fit. As parents listen to and talk with their children and elaborate on ideas, children feel more a part of the reading process. They also can begin to make their own connections to the text, leading to a more complete understanding of what is being read.

Using the Adult–Child Interactive Reading Inventory

This chapter prepares the reader to implement the ACIRI and to understand how to use the ACIRI for program and professional development. The following issues are clarified:

- Uses of the ACIRI
- How to set up the environment
- How to prepare the adult and child for the assessment
- Administration of the ACIRI
- Directions for scoring the ACIRI
- Establishment of reliability
- Definitions of ACIRI behaviors
- The ACIRI and program development
- The ACIRI and professional development

USES OF THE ADULT–CHILD INTERACTIVE READING INVENTORY

The ACIRI can be used in center-, school-, or home-based programs. It is most typically used with a parent or caregiver and a child 3–5 years old. It has also been used with both older and younger children. It has been helpful in the training of tutors, student teachers, and other volunteers who read with young children. Using the ACIRI can assist in providing specific professional development related to interactive reading.

The ACIRI also has been translated into Spanish so that it can be easily shared with adults whose first language is Spanish (see Section II). When a bilingual teacher uses the ACIRI with Spanish-speaking families, he or she commonly uses a children's book written in Spanish as well. If the adult and child speak a language other than English and Spanish, and the teacher speaks the same language, a book written in the native language of the family is best if one is available. The teacher can then translate his or her comments and explanations into the language understood by the adult.

SETTING UP THE ENVIRONMENT

The most important requirement for administering the ACIRI is that it be done in a quiet place without distraction. In addition, the person administering the ACIRI should never stare at the pair reading, as this can cause them to feel uncomfortable and self-conscious. He or she sits to the back and to the side of them where their faces and the book can be observed without intrusion.

PREPARING THE ADULT AND CHILD FOR THE ADULT–CHILD INTERACTIVE READING INVENTORY

Ensuring that the adult and the child feel comfortable when the ACIRI is being used is very important. When the teacher explains what will occur when the ACIRI is used, he or she needs to present it as a method for helping parents/caregivers improve their interactive reading skills:

> Today, I am going to watch you read with your child. I will be right behind you. I know you do wonderful things when you read, and I want to write down some of these things as well as others that can help you improve on so your child can become a successful reader. When you are done, I will share everything I have written.

It is valuable for parents/caregivers to understand that interactive reading that includes particular behaviors and strategies can assist young children in gaining the early literacy skills that lead them to become effective readers and succeed in school. This is a highly motivating reason for a parent to want to participate in this evaluation.

ADMINISTRATION OF THE ADULT–CHILD INTERACTIVE READING INVENTORY

When used for program evaluation purposes, the ACIRI was designed to be implemented in the fall (pretest) and then again in the spring (posttest). Each administration of the ACIRI takes 15–20 minutes. The length of time spent depends on the complexity of the book being read and the number of observed behaviors the teacher wishes to discuss with the adult following the observation. Before the teacher implements the ACIRI, he or she fills in the blanks in the box on the Scoring Sheet on the back of the tool and checks whether the test is pre or post. This information needs to be filled out before the scores are recorded and should not be done in front of the adult. The procedures for using the ACIRI are as follows.

Step 1: Selecting a Book

The adult, child, and teacher select an age-appropriate book from the variety of books the teacher brings with him or her. The teacher has chosen in advance books that match the child's developmental level and the adult's reading level. These books can be representative of specific cultures or in languages other than English provided the teacher is fluent in the family's home language. Wordless picture books may also be used, permitting adults who are English-language learners and children and adults with low conventional literacy skills to participate.

Step 2: Observing Interactive Reading

The adult and child read together while being observed by their teacher, who sits behind and to the side of them so as not to stare. The teacher notes adult and child behaviors on the inventory and writes comments as the reading progresses. The teacher should note some exact questions or comments to personalize the conversation that takes place after the assessment is completed. Tick marks also can be used on the observation sheet to keep track of the frequency of a specific behavior, such as the number of times an adult asks a child a question.

Step 3: Sharing Feedback

When the reading is complete, the teacher briefly studies his or her comments and then discusses them with the adult in a nonthreatening, helpful manner, using the inventory as a teaching tool, thus linking teaching directly to assessment. The adult can follow along with the teacher, allowing the ACIRI to be an open and shared evaluation. When the teacher reviews the ACIRI with the adult, he or she may find it useful to use sandwich imagery: to sandwich a suggestion for improvement between two positive comments. If the adult's first language is Spanish, the teacher can share the inventory in the same open manner by using the Spanish version. As this conversation is taking place, the child can sit nearby and either read a book provided by the teacher, color a picture, or go back to class and work on an activity provided by the teacher if the ACIRI is done.

Step 4: Scoring the Observations

After completing the assessment and conversation with the adult and after the teacher or the adult and child leave, the teacher reads over his or her comments and numerically scores the behaviors privately, entering the scores in the appropriate columns on the Scoring Sheet on the back of the tool. The numerical scores are used for program evaluation purposes only and are not meant to be shared with participants. The goal in using the ACIRI with families is to be encouraging, friendly, and nonthreatening. Numerical scores can

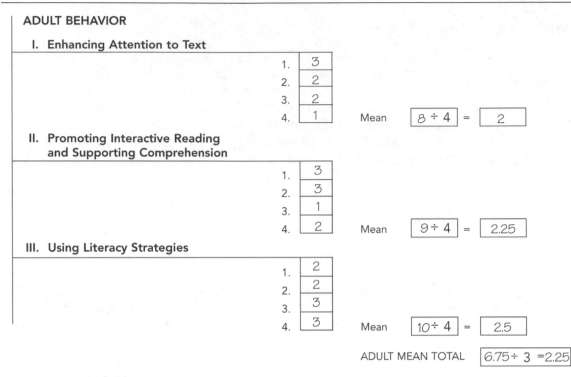

ADULT BEHAVIOR

I. Enhancing Attention to Text

1.	3
2.	2
3.	2
4.	1

Mean $8 \div 4$ = 2

II. Promoting Interactive Reading and Supporting Comprehension

1.	3
2.	3
3.	1
4.	2

Mean $9 \div 4$ = 2.25

III. Using Literacy Strategies

1.	2
2.	2
3.	3
4.	3

Mean $10 \div 4$ = 2.5

ADULT MEAN TOTAL $6.75 \div 3 = 2.25$

Figure 1. Example of adult score.

only serve to associate the ACIRI with a testing rather than a teaching situation, and this creates discomfort in the majority of participants.

DIRECTIONS FOR SCORING THE ADULT–CHILD INTERACTIVE READING INVENTORY

The ACIRI can be quantitatively scored for program evaluation purposes. Qualitative data in the form of written comments are also available to support numerical scores and provide teachers with a detailed picture of what occurred during the reading interaction.

Numerical Scoring

The numerical scoring is based on a 0–3 scale as follows:

- 0 indicates *no evidence* of the behavior (0 times)
- 1 indicates that the behavior occurs *infrequently* (1 time)
- 2 indicates that the behavior occurs *some of the time* (2–3 times)
- 3 indicates that the behavior occurs *most of the time* (4 or more times)

Adult and child reading behaviors are separately indicated by scores on each individual item, by mean scores on the three broad categories, and by the total mean score of the inventory for the adult and for the child. To obtain the mean score for each category, add together the four individual behavior scores for the adult and divide the total by 4 to get the mean for each category; do the same for the child. To obtain the adult mean score for the entire inventory, add together the three mean category scores for the adult and divide by 3; do the same for the child (see Figure 3.1). Pre- and posttest scores can then be compared to demonstrate progress.

Observational Notes

As mentioned previously, the teacher makes observational notes near each listed behavior as he or she sees it occur. These qualitative data assist the teacher in quantitatively scoring the inventory when the reading ends.

Because of space limitations on the tool as well as the need to pay more attention to the adult and child reading than to writing comments, teachers need to use abbreviated comments and other shortcuts for scoring. Tick marks can be used to keep track of number of questions asked and coordinated responses, number of times a child predicts or recalls, and number of times an adult or child relates the story to their lives.

Because the teacher needs to recall specific examples of many of the behaviors he or she observes in order to provide the adult with useful and constructive feedback, having some abbreviated examples to share is also important. If the adult is reading a book about Clifford the big red dog, and Clifford is going to the park with his friends, the child (C) might say, "I go to the park with my friends, too." The adult (A) might respond, "Yes, I take you every Saturday morning." The teacher could note that as: park, friends (C), Sat AM (A). This would remind the teacher of what was said to demonstrate relating the book to personal experiences on both the part of the adult and the child.

Establishing Reliability

Before the ACIRI can be used effectively, teachers must be very familiar with the definitions of the behaviors explained in the next section, understand the scoring system, and be able to score consistently. The scoring system is carefully defined below. To establish reliability in scoring, a series of three videotaped or live interactive reading sessions should be observed and scored by those who will be administering the ACIRI. After each dyad is observed, the person responsible for leading the group should go over the behaviors on the ACIRI one by one with those who scored. Whenever there is a disagreement in scoring, a discussion should ensue to find out why and an attempt should be made to reach agreement using the behavior definitions provided. The objective of establishing reliability is to be sure that everyone using the tool scores it in the same way. Having multiple people rate the same dyad provides the opportunity to ensure this happens.

DEFINITIONS OF ADULT–CHILD INTERACTIVE READING INVENTORY BEHAVIORS

Anyone using the ACIRI must have a comprehensive understanding of the following definitions before implementing assessment or related curriculum. These definitions were created to be informative and to assist in the establishment of reliability and the stability or consistency of scoring by a variety of people. If evaluators do not agree on definitions of the behaviors that they are observing, the results will not be reliable or useful. Please note that these definitions represent the ideal behavior (e.g., a score of 3 on the ACIRI).

Adult Categories and Behaviors

The categories and behaviors for adults using the ACIRI were determined by thoroughly examining research on interactive reading. The first category, Enhancing Attention to Text, represents research in the areas of attachment (Bus, 2001), book-handling skills (Clay, 1985, 1993), and motivation and interest (Baker & Scher, 2002; Sperling & Head, 2002). The second category, Promoting Interactive Reading and Supporting Comprehension, reflects research in the fields of questioning (Flood, 1977; Smolkin & Donovan, 2002) and comprehension (Martinez, 1983; Morrow, 1989). The third category, Using Literacy Strategies, focuses on research on identification (Yaden, Smolkin, & Conlin, 1989) and comprehension, specifically prediction, retelling, and elaboration (Cornell, Senechal, & Brodo, 1988; Martin, 1998; Paris & Paris, 2003).

Each category and each behavior is written to be developmentally sensitive (Neuman, Copple, & Bredekamp, 1999; Snow et al., 1998). In addition, affect is a prominent component (e.g., the use of different character voices and relating real-life experiences to the content of the book). An important component of the entire tool or inventory is the development of listening skills and wait time on the part of the parent/guardian. In order for interactive reading to be a learning experience as well as a joyful one, parents/guardians must learn to listen to what their children are saying spontaneously or in response to questions or comments. Sometimes listening requires wait time—giving the child a reasonable time to speak rather than speaking for him or her if an answer is not given promptly. The adult categories and behaviors are as follows:

I. Enhancing Attention to Text

1. **Adult attempts to promote and maintain physical proximity with the child.**

   The adult makes an effort to sit in close proximity to the child as the adult prepares to and continues to read to the child. This includes inviting the child to sit on the adult's lap or within a close enough distance so that both individuals can see the book and interact.

2. **Adult sustains the child's interest and attention through use of child-adjusted language, positive affect, and reinforcement.**

   The adult is able to keep the child's interest by using an animated, engaging voice, perhaps speaking in a variety of voices that are representative of the storybook's characters, simplifying language when necessary, maintaining a positive attitude about the storybook and reading it together, and pausing during reading to encourage the child to respond to the text or the adult's comments.

3. **Adult gives the child an opportunity to hold the book and turn pages.**

The adult begins the book-reading session by allowing the child to assist in holding the book, or if the child is old enough, hold the book on his or her own. The adult also encourages the child to turn the pages at the appropriate times. Sometimes the child may wish to turn the pages in a way that demonstrates he or she is not paying attention to the story. The adult gently works with the child to assist him or her in turning the pages so as to follow the story.

4. **Adult shares the book with the child (displays sense of audience in book handling when reading).**

The adult considers the child's developmental level, physical size, possible disabilities, fine motor skills, language capabilities, and personal interests when sharing a book with him or her. The adult shares the book so the child feels like an active part of the dyad, not just a passive member. It is important for the child to see the text and pictures and touch or hold the book if he or she wishes.

II. Promoting Interactive Reading and Supporting Comprehension

1. **Adult poses and solicits questions about the book's content.**

The adult looks for places in the book where he or she can pose relevant questions to the child, questions that will ask the child to reflect on what has been read. The adult also frequently asks the child if he or she has any questions. This most often will be done by referring directly to book content. It is important for the adult to ask questions that go beyond just seeking information (e.g., questions about plot, questions about characters' feelings, "why" and "how" questions).

2. **Adult points to pictures and words to assist the child in identification and understanding.**

The adult often points to pictures and words in the text to assist the child in identifying them and learning their meaning. How often the adult points to pictures versus words and also the complexity of the chosen words are determined by the adult's understanding of the child's developmental level. Many books have repetitive words or phrases that a child can easily begin to identify and "read."

3. **Adult relates the book's content and the child's responses to personal experiences.**

The adult puts forth great effort to make the content of the book relevant to the child's life experiences. In addition, he or she carefully listens to comments that the child makes as the book is being read and attempts to relate the comments to the content of the book.

4. **Adult pauses to answer questions that the child poses.**

The adult is careful to stop reading the book when the child poses a question. The adult makes every attempt to answer the question or to pose further questions to the child so he or she can discover an answer on his or her own.

III. Using Literacy Strategies

1. **Adult identifies visual cues related to story reading (e.g., pictures, repetitive words).**

The adult identifies visual cues for the child that will assist him or her in following and understanding the story. In many books, the authors use repetitive words or phrases throughout a book to signal what will come next. Pictures are often clues to the storyline, and even children who cannot read can feel like readers if they learn to recognize these cues.

2. **Adult solicits predictions.**

The adult looks for places in the story to stop and ask the child what the child thinks will happen next in the story or to a specific character. The adult should get excited along with the child as the child makes these predictions and should give the child credit for use of his or her imagination.

3. **Adult asks the child to recall information from the story.**

The adult stops during the reading of the book and asks the child to recall or summarize information from the story. This assists the adult in recognizing the child's level of comprehension. If the child cannot recall information, then the adult can turn back pages and review the story with the child in a pleasant manner (e.g., "Remember when…").

4. **Adult elaborates on the child's ideas.**

The adult always tries to elaborate on the child's ideas, no matter how silly or unrelated they may appear. Asking questions, finding ways to make the child's comments relate to something that the adult or child knows, and knowing how to guide the child in connecting these ideas to the story all are important strategies the adult can use to elaborate on a child's ideas.

Child Categories and Behaviors

The child categories and behaviors are based on the same research used for adults using the ACIRI. Adult and child behaviors are linked, thus making the ACIRI an interactive evaluation tool. The differences are, of course, developmental in nature (i.e., what a child can do in response to what an adult is doing). The child categories and behaviors are as follows.

I. Enhancing Attention to Text

1. **Child seeks and maintains physical proximity.**

    The child wants to be close to the adult and attempts to sit close to him or her either by climbing on the adult's lap or sitting close enough to see the book and turn the pages. The child remains close during the entire reading of the story.

2. **Child pays attention and sustains interest.**

    The child is interested in the story and pays attention to the reader. He or she is rarely distracted and is engaged in listening and motivated to interact with the adult.

3. **Child holds the book and turns the pages on his or her own or when asked.**

    The child is eager to hold the book and turn the pages when the adult offers the opportunity. The child may also spontaneously do this; however, if the child grabs the book and turns pages randomly, not really following the story or allowing it to be read, this is not a desired behavior.

4. **Child initiates or responds to book sharing that takes his or her presence into account.**

    The child may ask the adult to read in character voices or to let him or her participate more in the shared book reading. The child may demonstrate a strong desire and interest in remaining a part of an interactive dyad due to the adult's ability to consider the child's developmental level, physical size, possible disabilities, fine motor skills, language capabilities, and personal interests when sharing a book with the child.

II. Promoting Interactive Reading and Supporting Comprehension

1. **Child responds to questions about the book.**

    The child answers questions that the adult asks him or her about the book. He or she is responsive and asks for more information if he or she doesn't understand the question. The child does not ignore questions and just push forward in the story.

2. **Child responds to adult cues or identifies pictures and words on his or her own.**

    The child is ready to respond to the cues that the adult provides in regard to picture and word identification. The child shows an understanding of the pictures and words that are called to his or her attention and may begin to pick them out on his or her own as the book progresses.

3. **Child attempts to relate the book's content to personal experiences.**

    The child looks for ways to make the content of the book relevant to his or her life experiences. For example, the child may associate something in the book with something he or she knows, has done, has seen on television or in another book, or has heard about from others.

4. **Child poses questions about the story and related topics.**

    The child asks questions as the book is read to clarify information, questions that are piqued by curiosity or even questions that demonstrate his or her ability to relate the content of the book to something he or she already knows.

III. Using Literacy Strategies

1. **Child responds to the adult and/or identifies visual cues related to the story him- or herself.**

    The child responds to the pictures, repetitive words, or other cues that the adult has pointed out. He or she is able to follow patterns in the story by eventually recognizing particular pictures or words independently as the story progresses.

2. **Child is able to guess what will happen next based on picture cues.**

    The child tries to predict what will happen next in the story on his or her own. He or she follows the story and, using his or her imagination as well as clues picked up from pictures or word patterns, guesses what is coming up in the story. This might be what will happen on the next page or even what the ending of the book will be.

3. **Child is able to recall information from the story.**

    The child is able to remember information from the story when asked by the adult. The complexity of this information is determined by the book's content and the child's developmental level.

4. **Child spontaneously offers ideas about the story.**

    The child volunteers ideas about the story as the reading progresses. He or she may do this at any time, usually when he or she is excited about something that has developed in the story or when he or she recognizes some information and wants to add to it.

Each of the adult and child behaviors previously listed provide a clear picture of what to look for when scoring the ACIRI. When observing the adult and child reading together, the teacher can see exactly which behaviors and strategies they are using. This provides a clear path to understanding what type of intervention is needed to assist in the areas that need improvement. In

Section III of this book, specific tips, activities, and lists of related books are provided that target each behavior on the ACIRI. This linked curriculum provides teachers with the tools needed to promote effective interactive reading.

USING THE ADULT–CHILD INTERACTIVE READING INVENTORY FOR PROGRAM DEVELOPMENT

Since it has been in use, the ACIRI has been shown to be sensitive to growth and change over time in interactive reading skills for both children and adults. It has proven useful to teachers as a measurement of adult and child reading behavior and progress (Boyce et al., 2004; DeBruin-Parecki, 1999; DeBruin-Parecki & Oak, 2005). It can provide a means to promote joint storybook reading and to observe the interactive behaviors of adults and children as they are engaged in this process. It provides quantitative information to satisfy those who require a numerical means of judging progress and qualitative data to enrich the numerical data and expand on the reasons for assigning certain scores. Qualitative data also provide teachers or test administrators with useful evidence to assist in explaining to adults what they saw during the observation. These same data can serve as examples for teachers to use in their family literacy programs. While programs are able to compile useful data to report to their policymakers, administrators, and funders to help ensure continued support, teachers are able to focus on the teaching and learning aspects of the tool.

Using time between tests and adult and child development as natural interventions as well as a curriculum directly linked to effective interactive reading practice, the ACIRI is meant to encourage good instruction as well as authentic and friendly assessment. It also helps teachers determine where to focus their efforts when it comes to promoting effective reading behaviors.

Two key goals of family literacy programs are improving the literacy skills of both adults and children and encouraging adults to practice reading behaviors in family settings with their youngsters that will enhance these children's ability to do well in school. As shown throughout this book, the behaviors listed in the inventory are supported by research that has demonstrated that the learning and practicing of these skills gives children a head start when they begin school, assists adults in improving their own skills, and further provides positive opportunities for families to interact around literacy together. These positive opportunities may help dispel any negative feelings adults may retain from their own school experiences.

The ACIRI enables teachers to ascertain which of the skills adults and children already practice, which permits teachers to design individualized instruction that will improve these skills and introduce others. Teachers also are able to use the inventory as a teaching tool by discussing with the adult the interactive reading behaviors observed during the session, how they can be imroved, and which skills the adult still needs to master. The design of this tool provides a unique means of authenticating the progress that adults and children are making as they learn to read together.

USING THE ADULT–CHILD INTERACTIVE
READING INVENTORY FOR PROFESSIONAL DEVELOPMENT

With the current emphasis on professional development for preschool teachers, tutors, and volunteers, this tool also can play an important role as a training tool to educate teachers and tutors about interactive reading skills. When using the ACIRI for training or professional development purposes in a one-to-one situation, the procedure for administration is the same. The adult (e.g., tutor, volunteer) and a child, or an adult role-playing a child, read a book together. After the ACIRI is administered, discussing the results allows teachers, volunteers, or tutors to focus on improving their low-scoring behaviors. Improving those specific behaviors can have a positive impact on future interactive reading sessions and assist teachers, volunteers, and tutors in planning more effective early literacy skill instruction. When possible, videotaping interactive reading sessions for sharing is an excellent idea. These videotapes can provide the stimulus for excellent collaborative learning conversations.

The teacher, volunteer, or tutor is evaluated preinstruction with an intervention of some type in between, such as one from Categories I, II, and III in this book. After the intervention, the teacher, volunteer, or tutor is evaluated again for improvement. The ACIRI can inform administrators of the skills of interactive reading teachers, tutors, volunteers, and so forth in their programs and provide these individuals with a road map for further professional development. Some programs may choose to use the ACIRI to promote learning of effective reading behaviors by observing and rating adults and children's progress on videotape or DVD.

USING THE ADULT–CHILD INTERACTIVE
READING BEHAVIORS TO CREATE A LINKED CURRICULUM

To encourage the adult to practice the behaviors on the ACIRI, there is a need for effective programs. These programs provide activities that are linked to the behaviors on the ACIRI for an adult to do in class and at home with his or her child. After the ACIRI is administered, the specific behaviors a particular adult and child need to master are easy to determine. This allows the teacher to either tailor a program to these individuals or to call on these individuals to act as role models and mentors in a larger class setting. Chapters 4, 5, and 6 provide tips to encourage adults to use each behavior with their children, activities supporting each behavior, and finally an annotated bibliography of children's books that help promote each behavior.

Adult–Child Interactive Reading Inventory (ACIRI)

aciri™ Adult–Child Interactive Reading Inventory

ADULT BEHAVIOR	OBSERVATION	CHILD BEHAVIOR	OBSERVATION
I. Enhancing Attention to Text		**I. Enhancing Attention to Text**	
1. Adult attempts to promote and maintain physical proximity with the child.		1. Child seeks and maintains physical proximity.	
2. Adult sustains interest and attention through use of child-adjusted language, positive affect, and reinforcement.		2. Child pays attention and sustains interest.	
3. Adult gives the child an opportunity to hold the book and turn pages.		3. Child holds the book and turns the pages on his or her own or when asked.	
4. Adult shares the book with the child (displays sense of audience in book handling when reading).		4. Child initiates or responds to book sharing that takes his or her presence into account.	
II. Promoting Interactive Reading and Supporting Comprehension		**II. Promoting Interactive Reading and Supporting Comprehension**	
1. Adult poses and solicits questions about the book's content.		1. Child responds to questions about the book.	
2. Adult points to pictures and words to assist the child in identification and understanding.		2. Child responds to adult cues or identifies pictures and words on his or her own.	
3. Adult relates the book's content and the child's responses to personal experiences.		3. Child attempts to relate the book's content to personal experiences.	
4. Adult pauses to answer questions that the child poses.		4. Child poses questions about the story and related topics.	
III. Using Literacy Strategies		**III. Using Literacy Strategies**	
1. Adult identifies visual cues related to story reading (e.g., pictures, repetitive words).		1. Child responds to the adult and/or identifies visual cues related to the story him- or herself.	
2. Adult solicits predictions.		2. Child is able to guess what will happen next based on picture cues.	
3. Adult asks the child to recall information from the story.		3. Child is able to recall information from the story.	
4. Adult elaborates on the child's ideas.		4. Child spontaneously offers ideas about the story.	

Let's Read Together: Improving Literacy Outcomes with the Adult–Child Interactive Reading Inventory by A. DeBruin-Parecki.

aciri™ Adult–Child Interactive Reading Inventory Scoring Sheet

Date of observation _____

Program _____

Teacher/observer _____

Adult name/case number _____

Age _____

Date of birth _____

Child name/case number _____

Age _____

Date of birth _____

Title of book _____

Author _____

Notes: _____

SCORE (0–3)

3 = most of the time (4 or more times)
2 = some of the time (2–3 times)
1 = infrequently (1 time)
0 = no evidence

Pre ☐
Post ☐

ADULT BEHAVIOR

I. Enhancing Attention to Text
1.
2.
3.
4.
Mean ▭ ÷ 4 = ▭

II. Promoting Interactive Reading and Supporting Comprehension
1.
2.
3.
4.
Mean ▭ ÷ 4 = ▭

III. Using Literacy Strategies
1.
2.
3.
4.
Mean ▭ ÷ 4 = ▭

ADULT MEAN TOTAL ▭ ÷ 3 = ▭

CHILD BEHAVIOR

I. Enhancing Attention to Text
1.
2.
3.
4.
Mean ▭ ÷ 4 = ▭

II. Promoting Interactive Reading and Supporting Comprehension
1.
2.
3.
4.
Mean ▭ ÷ 4 = ▭

III. Using Literacy Strategies
1.
2.
3.
4.
Mean ▭ ÷ 4 = ▭

CHILD MEAN TOTAL ▭ ÷ 3 = ▭

aciri™ Inventario de Lectura Interactiva Adulto–Niño

CONDUCTAS DEL ADULTO	OBSERVACIONES	CONDUCTAS DEL NIÑO	OBSERVACIONES
I. Dirige la atención hacia el texto		**I. Dirige la atención hacia el texto**	
1. Trata de promover y mantener proximidad física con el niño.		1. El niño busca y mantiene proximidad física.	
2. Mantiene interés y atención a través del uso de lenguaje apropiado al niño, afectividad positiva y refuerzos.		2. El niño presta atención y mantiene su interés.	
3. Permite que el niño tome el libro y dé vuelta las páginas.		3. El niño toma el libro y da vuelta las páginas por su cuenta o cuando se le pide.	
4. Comparte el libro con el niño (demuestra tener sentido de quién es la audiencia cuando manipula el libro).		4. El niño toma la iniciativa de tomar el libro o responde cuando se quiere compartir el libro con él.	
II. Promueva la lectura interactiva y apoya la comprensión		**II. Promueva la lectura interactiva y apoya la comprensión**	
1. Hace y solicita preguntas con respecto a los contenidos de la lectura.		1. El niño responde a preguntas con respecto a los contenidos de la lectura.	
2. Señala dibujos y palabras para apoyar al niño en la identificación y comprensión.		2. El niño responde a claves dadas por el adulto e identifica dibujos y palabras por su cuenta.	
3. Relaciona con experiencias personales los contenidos de la lectura y las respuestas del niño.		3. El niño trata de relacionar sus experiencias personales con los contenidos de la lectura.	
4. Se toma tiempo para responder a las preguntas del niño.		4. El niño hace preguntas sobre la lectura y temas relacionados.	
III. Usa estrategias de alfabetización		**III. Usa estrategias de alfabetización**	
1. Identifica claves visuales relacionadas con la lectura de cuentos (ej. dibujos, palabras repetidas).		1. El niño responde al adulto y/o toma iniciativa en identificar claves visuales relacionadas con la lectura.	
2. Solicita predicciones.		2. En base a claves visuales, el niño es capaz de adivinar lo que pasará más adelante.	
3. Le pide al niño que se acuerde de la información presentada en el cuento.		3. El niño puede recordar la información presentada en el cuento.	
4. Explica en detalle las ideas del niño.		4. El niño elabora espontáneamente ideas sobre el cuento.	

Let's Read Together: Improving Literacy Outcomes with the Adult–Child Interactive Reading Inventory by A. DeBruin-Parecki. © 2007 Brookes Publishing Co., Inc. All rights reserved.

aciri™ Inventario de Lectura Interactiva Adulto–Niño Hoja de Puntaje

Fecha de elaboración _____

Programa _____

Maestro/observador _____

Nombre del adulto/número de caso _____

Edad _____

Fecha de nacimiento _____

Nombre del niño/número de caso _____

Edad _____

Fecha de nacimiento _____

Título del libro _____

Autor _____

Observaciones: _____

PUNTAJE (0–3)

3 = la mayor parte del tiempo (4 o más veces)
2 = parte del tiempo (2–3 veces)
1 = rara vez
0 = no hay datos

Pre ☐

Post ☐

CONDUCTAS DEL ADULTO

I. Dirige atención hacia el texto
1.
2.
3.
4.
Promedio [ ] ÷ 4 = [ ]

II. Promueve la lectura interactiva y apoya la comprensión
1.
2.
3.
4.
Promedio [ ] ÷ 4 = [ ]

III. Usa estrategias de alfabetización
1.
2.
3.
4.
Promedio [ ] ÷ 4 = [ ]

PROMEDIO TOTAL DEL ADULTO [ ] ÷ 3 = [ ]

CONDUCTAS DEL NIÑO

I. Dirige atención hacia el texto
1.
2.
3.
4.
Promedio [ ] ÷ 4 = [ ]

II. Promueve la lectura interactiva y apoya la comprensión
1.
2.
3.
4.
Promedio [ ] ÷ 4 = [ ]

III. Usa estrategias de alfabetización
1.
2.
3.
4.
Promedio [ ] ÷ 4 = [ ]

PROMEDIO TOTAL DEL NIÑO [ ] ÷ 3 = [ ]

Linked Activities to Foster Family Literacy

Each category in this section begins with research that supports the specific behaviors of the category as it appears on the Adult–Child Interactive Reading Inventory. Following this research, each behavior in the category is presented separately accompanied by tips to encourage that behavior. These tips can be shared with adults when trying to teach them to put these behaviors into practice during interactive reading sessions. In addition to the tips are activities to use with adults and children both in class and at home that emphasize each specific behavior. These printable and photocopiable activities and activity sheets are available both in English and in Spanish in full color on the CD-ROM in the back of this book. Annotated lists of children's books that strengthen the use of each of these behaviors also are included. When books are available in Spanish, this is noted.

This section provides teachers and administrators with a framework for creating a family literacy or parent involvement program based on interactive reading skills development. By linking curriculum directly to assessment, a program can be sure that they are individualizing instruction to family needs and are fairly evaluating each family's progress by testing them on material they have actually been taught and have put into practice.

One way to model the tips is to use puppets. Using puppets is a way to get the information to the adults in a nonthreatening manner and is also fun for the children. The activities that follow the modeling of the tips are used to develop and practice the reading strategies presented in the puppet show. Books from the recommended reading books list for each behavior are appropriate for the puppets to model. Some programs may prefer to have adults in the class role-play these modeled behaviors while reading.

When planning for the activities, the instructor should remember to supply materials whenever possible. Instructors often assume that families have even the simplest supplies when in fact they may not have them. Grants are ways to obtain money to supply the materials for the classes and should be researched approximately a year before getting a program running. Many organizations are willing to donate money for programs similar to these. Although organizations may be willing to donate, however, many companies have specific times of the year that they distribute money. Local businesses and larger corporations alike may be willing to donate money. Other places may allow the program to be held at their site for a small fee or no fee. Some businesses may donate supplies. Regardless, many families truly cannot afford supplies for a class like this, so having them on hand is a necessity.

The program size can vary, but 15 families is an ideal number for one or two instructors. The instructors have difficulty giving individual families attention when there are too many participants. Each program may have many different families. Mothers, fathers, grandmothers, grandfathers, aunts, uncles, or other caregivers may choose to participate. Participants should include one adult per child, and that adult needs to be with the child consistently throughout the program. That consistency is necessary to maximize the effect of the program for both parties. Ideally, the child should be between the ages of 3 and 6 years old. Children younger than 3 typically cannot focus as long, and children older than 6 are out of the early childhood focus of the program. Although the maturity differences among the children may differ, the positive interaction between the dyads and getting the dyads to learn how to read together and enjoy it are the primary goals.

When planning the program, scheduling is important. Picking a time and day of the week that is ideal for your target participants is necessary. That will vary by location. An appropriate amount of time for each of the sessions is from 1 hour to 1 hour, 15 minutes. Purchasing materials for the program also needs to be done in advance. General art supplies such as scissors, glue sticks, paper, crayons, markers, binders for take-home activities, and similar items are needed. Finding the appropriate books and locating sufficient quantities also take advance planning and time. Libraries often can be of great assistance to programs. Books to give to the families each week are important so families can practice the strategies at home. In all of the activities that follow, the teacher will always model the activity before asking adults and children to do it in class or at home.

Enhancing Attention to Text

with Adam Severson

In the following pages, each behavior is presented along with tips to encourage adults to practice the behavior while reading with their children, related activities, and books to support the development of the behavior. Specifically, the activities and behaviors in this chapter are designed to help adults direct the child toward text in the story. These are the beginning steps in improving the interaction and effectiveness of adult and child storybook reading.

BEHAVIORS IN CATEGORY I

BEHAVIOR 1: Maintaining Physical Proximity

BEHAVIOR 2: Sustaining Interest and Attention

BEHAVIOR 3: Holding the Book and Turning Pages

BEHAVIOR 4: Displaying a Sense of Audience

Maintaining Physical Proximity

BEHAVIOR

1

Maintaining Physical Proximity

- Adult attempts to promote and maintain physical proximity with the child.

- Child seeks and maintains physical proximity.

This behavior can be shown by the child sitting on the adult's lap or right next to the adult so the two are touching.

PARENT/CAREGIVER TIPS FOR BEHAVIOR 1

- Find a quiet, comfortable place to read with your child.

- Encourage your child to sit on your lap.

- Make sure your child is close to you.

CLASS ACTIVITY

Read Aloud

Purpose:

To give the dyads an opportunity to bond and practice being in close physical proximity while reading

Process:

1. The teacher gives a short introduction to the book that gives the dyads some background on why physical proximity is important in helping children to become readers.

2. The adult and child are asked to find a comfortable place to sit.

3. The adult is encouraged to sit close to the child or have the child sit on his or her lap.

Materials needed:

4. The adult and child are given an opportunity to read the book together for approximately 10–15 minutes. If the dyad finishes early, they may choose to go back through the book looking at the pictures in more detail.

○ *I Love My Little Storybook* by Anita Jeram (which allows adults and children to see cozy reading situations) or a book from the list of recommended books for this behavior

5. The teacher walks around the room to offer any help that might be needed.

6. When the adult and child have completed the reading, they share their ideas about the story. For example, the dyads could share what they liked, what pictures were the best, or any comments about keeping in close proximity.

○ "Where Did You Read to Your Child this Week?" activity sheet

7. At the conclusion of this activity, the adult and child are asked to draw pictures of where they read together now. Then, the "Where Did You Read to Your Child this Week?" take-home activity sheet is sent home for the adult and child to fill out for discussion the following week.

○ _____

○ _____

○ _____

Maintaining Physical Proximity

Where Did You Read with
Your Child This Week?

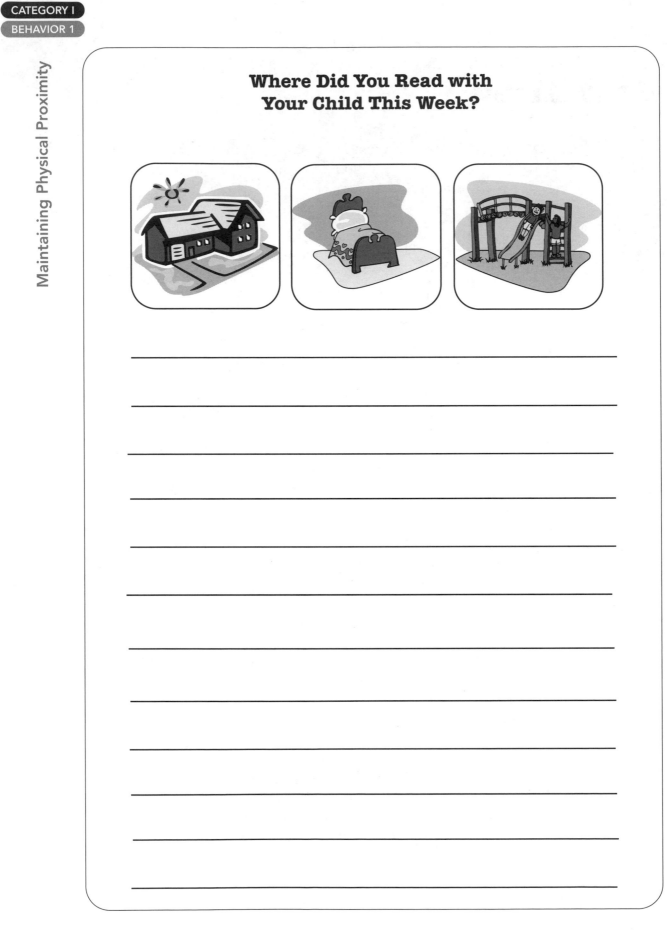

_____

_____

_____

_____

_____

_____

_____

_____

_____

TAKE-HOME ACTIVITY

Trust Walk

Purpose: To promote physical proximity between the adult and child in each dyad

Process:

1. Find a safe place for you and your child to begin this activity.

2. Place a blindfold over the child's eyes.

3. Take the child's hand and lead him or her along a path inside or outside that was picked earlier by you.

4. Carefully describe what is seen.

5. Ask your child if he or she can guess what might be coming up or describe things in detail.

6. After the walk is over, remove the blindfold.

7. Sit close to the child while he or she draws some of the things described during the walk.

8. You can help remind the child of details if asked. After the drawing is over, review the walk through the pictures.

9. Bring your child's drawing to class next week to share with others.

Materials needed:

○ handkerchief

○ paper

○ crayons or markers

○ _____

○ _____

○ _____

51

Recommended Books

The following books all are ideal books to promote physical proximity between adults and children. Each book describes different relationships between adults and children. Some relationships are between animals, but the idea is still the same. Although most picture books will help adults and children practice proximity, these books were chosen because of the focus on family relationships.

Cusimano, M. (2001). *You are my I love you.* **New York: Philomel.**

Love between a parent and child is shown as they go through a typical day. This rhyming story depicts parents and children working to get along on a daily basis.

Jeram, A. (2002). *I love my little storybook.* **Cambridge, MA: Candlewick Press.**

A young bunny is looking at his first storybook. This wonderful experience has the young bunny in awe of everything on the pages, but what he loves most about the story is the amazing characters throughout the storybook. This book is also available in Spanish as *Me Gusta Mi Libro De Cuentos.*

Parr, T. (2002). *The daddy book.* **New York: Megan Tingley Books.**

Working at home, working far away, with hair, missing hair, camping, buying things—Daddies do many different things and look different in many ways. This book contains wonderful illustrations to help show many different types of fathers.

Parr, T. (2002). *The mommy book.* **New York: Megan Tingley Books.**

Many different mommies are shown throughout the book. Some mommies have short hair, some have long hair. Even though all mommies in the book are different, they all love their children.

Reiser, L. (1998). *Tortillas and lullabies/Tortillas y cancioncitas.* **New York: HarperCollins.**

A wonderful book about love and family customs over the years. It is filled with beautiful, colorful pictures and includes the music to a lullaby. Written in both Spanish and English.

Yolen, J. (2000). *How do dinosaurs say goodnight?* **New York: Scholastic.**

A mother and her child wonder about different ways a dinosaur can say goodnight. Eleven different dinosaur children are shown with different expressions. A dinosaur child is shown progressing from slamming his tail and pouting to giving a big hug and kiss to his parent in this humorous book.

BEHAVIOR 2

Sustaining Interest and Attention

- Adult sustains interest and attention through use of child-adjusted language, positive affect, and reinforcement.

- Child pays attention and sustains interest.

PARENT/CAREGIVER TIPS FOR BEHAVIOR 2

- Give your child compliments, and say when something is done well. For example, compliments could be given if the child points out a word or makes a connection to a picture in a book. Make these compliments specific (e.g., "I like the way you were able to show me the picture of the dog that looks like our dog").

- Be sure that your child feels part of the reading when you read together. The child should be able to touch the book and interject thoughts about the book.

- Change your voice to show what is going on in the book and to get and keep your child's attention. Give the characters in the book different voices. Use pauses at funny or dramatic parts of the book. Read softer or louder depending on the way the book is progressing.

- Use words you are sure your child knows as you talk and read through the book. Encourage your child to ask if he or she does not understand something you say or something from the book.

53

Sustaining Interest and Attention

CLASS ACTIVITY

Telling a Story Together

 Purpose: To allow dyads to practice positive interactions and the adults to speak at a level appropriate for the children

Process:

1. The teacher explains *and demonstrates* the activity.

2. The teacher instructs the dyads to find a comfortable place in the room where the adult and child can sit close to each other.

3. Together, the adult and child go through the wordless picture book. The adult needs to be sure to let the child hold the book and turn the pages.

4. As the dyad goes through the book, they "tell" the story together. The adult needs to be sure to use language that the child can understand.

5. The child then takes a turn telling the story to the adult.

6. When the dyads are finished (after about 10–15 minutes), the teacher gets the class back together and asks if a dyad would like to share their story with the group.

7. The teacher asks a dyad to model the "I Spy" game for the take-home activity.

Materials needed:

○ *A Boy, a Dog, and a Frog* or any book in this series by Mercer Mayer

○ _____

○ _____

○ _____

54

Sustaining Interest and Attention

TAKE-HOME ACTIVITY

I Spy

Purpose: To practice using language a child can understand and engage the child in the book

Process:

1. Using the book *Cloudy with a Chance of Meatballs,* play "I Spy" with your child. (You can try creating similar activities with other books from the Recommended Books list.)

2. Show your child how to play the game. The idea is to tell about something you see in the book by giving hints. You would say something like "I spy something alive." Your child would then form guesses such as "Is it an animal?" or "Is it furry?" until the right answer is guessed.

3. Switch roles with your child.

4. The two of you could play "I Spy" two or three times as you read through the book together.

Materials needed:

○ *Cloudy with a Chance of Meatballs* by Ron and Judy Barrett

○ _____

○ _____

○ _____

Recommended Books

The following books have been recommended because children find them interesting. Illustrations in the books are perfect for discussions. Children will remain interested and adults will have an opportunity to practice involving the children in the book.

Barrett, J. (1982). *Cloudy with a chance of meatballs.* **New York: Simon & Schuster.**

Chewandswallow is a town where food rains from the sky at breakfast, lunch, and supper. Everything is great until the raining food gets out of control. Everyone must evacuate the town!

Cronin, D. (2000). *Click, clack, moo: Cows that type.* **New York: Simon & Schuster.**

Farmer Brown starts to hear strange things in his barn. His very intelligent cows are tired of their working conditions, so they begin leaving him notes and bargaining for things. The next thing Farmer Brown knows, other animals have sided with the cows and a strike is planned. This book is also available in Spanish as *Clic, Clac, Muu: Vacas Escritotias.*

Kotzwinkle, W., & Murray, G. (2001). *Walter, the farting dog.* **Berkeley, CA: Frog Ltd.**

Walter is a dog with a farting problem. His family is about fed up with the smell and is close to taking him to the pound. When a burglar breaks in, Walter saves the day and earns his keep.

Long, M. (2003). *How I became a pirate.* **San Diego: Harcourt.**

Jeremy Jacob goes to the beach with his family and ends up recruited to help a peg-legged pirate named Braid Beardip bury treasure. The pirates' bad manners and lifestyle appeal to Jeremy at first, but then a storm hits and the pirates offer no comfort. Finally, the treasure is buried and Jeremy is returned to his parents.

Mayer, M. (2003). *A boy, a dog, and a frog.* **New York: Dial.**

A boy and a dog are out to catch a frog. However, they have a difficult time doing so. This wordless picture book allows the reader to tell the story as the book is read.

Rathmann, P. (1994). *Good night, Gorilla.* **New York: Putnam.**

A mischievous gorilla gets out of his cage at night and along with friends follows the zookeeper home. This book is also available in Spanish as *Buenas Noches, Gorilla.*

Wiesner, D. (1997). *Tuesday.* **Boston: Houghton Mifflin.**

It is Tuesday night. Frogs are out and suddenly flying through the air. This wordless picture book will allow the reader to tell the story as the pages are turned.

Williams, V.B. (1994). *A chair for my mother.* **New York: Greenwillow Books.**

When a fire destroys their belongings, a young girl, her mother, and her grandmother save their money for a much-deserved easy chair. This book is also available in Spanish as *Un Sillón Para Mi Mamá.*

BEHAVIOR 3

Holding the Book and Turning Pages

- Adult gives the child an opportunity to hold the book and turn the pages.

- Child holds the book and turns the pages on his or her own when asked.

PARENT/CAREGIVER TIPS FOR BEHAVIOR 3

- Let your child hold the book.

- Let your child turn the pages when he or she wants.

- Ask your child if he or she would like to turn the pages.

CLASS ACTIVITY

Mouse Hunt

Purpose: To give the dyads an opportunity to share a book and allow the child in each dyad to turn the pages

Process:

1. As they read *Cows in the Kitchen*, the adult and child go on a mouse hunt through the book looking for the mouse that appears in each scene of the book. (You can try creating similar activities with other books from the Recommended Books list.)

2. While the dyad goes through the book, the child holds the book and turns the pages while the adult reads each page and helps look for the mouse.

3. At the conclusion of this activity, the "Animals Should Definitely NOT Wear Clothing!" take-home activity could be described for discussion the following week.

Materials needed:

○ *Cows in the Kitchen* by June Crebbin

○ _____

○ _____

○ _____

Animals Wearing Clothing

Purpose: To give the adult and child a chance to share the book and to give the child a chance to turn the pages and anticipate what is ahead

Process:

1. Read *Animals Should Definitely Not Wear Clothing* to your child. (You can try creating similar activities with other books from the Recommended Books list.)

2. As the two of you go through the book, let your child hold the book and turn the pages.

3. When the story is done, both you and your child draw a picture of an animal wearing clothing on the activity sheet.

Materials needed:

○ *Animals Should Definitely Not Wear Clothing* by Judi Barrett

○ "Animals Should Definitely NOT Wear Clothing!" activity sheet

○ crayons or markers

○

○

○

Holding the Book and Turning Pages

59

Holding the Book and Turning Pages

Animals Should Definitely NOT Wear Clothing!

What would an animal look
like wearing clothes?
Can you draw one?

Recommended Books

Any book is fine for allowing children to turn the pages. These books were chosen because they capture and sustain a child's interest. The adult should feel free to allow and encourage the child to turn the pages of the book.

Barrett, J. (1989). *Animals should definitely not wear clothing.* **New York: Simon & Schuster.**

Pictures of animals wearing clothing show why they really shouldn't. Most animals just aren't built for wearing clothes. This book is also available in Spanish as *Los Animales No Se Visten.*

Boynton, S. (1982). *Moo, baa, la la la.* **New York: Workman.**

Animals are the focus of this silly story. This board book is highly entertaining for young children and parents alike.

Boynton, S. (1995). *Doggies.* **New York: Workman.**

Doggies have many different kinds of barks. This silly board book goes through them and is wonderful for adults to read with children.

Boynton, S. (1997). *Snoozers: 7 short bedtime stories for lively little kids.* **New York: Workman.**

Seven short, short stories are sure to entertain a child before bedtime. Finger tabs allow the child to flip through the book to different stories.

Boynton, S. (2003). *Snuggle puppy.* **New York: Workman.**

This board book is focused on love shared between a parent and child. Written in a sing-song style, the book is great for a parent and child to share. The artwork throughout the book easily will keep a child's interest.

Crebbins, J. (1998). *Cows in the kitchen.* **Cambridge, MA: Candlewick Press.**

Cows are in the kitchen. Ducks are in the dishes. Read to find out what will happen next with Tom Farmer's crazy farm!

Rathmann, P. (1994). *Good night, Gorilla.* **New York: Putnam.**

A mischievous gorilla gets out of his cage at night and along with friends follows the zookeeper home. This book is also available in Spanish as *Buenas Noches, Gorilla.*

Displaying a Sense of Audience

BEHAVIOR 4 Displaying a Sense of Audience

- Adult shares the book with the child (displays sense of audience in book handling when reading).

- Child initiates or responds to book sharing that takes his or her presence into account.

PARENT/CAREGIVER TIPS FOR BEHAVIOR 4

- Read your child stories.

- Have your child read you stories. This can include telling stories that go along with the pictures even if specific words can't be read by the child.

- Make sure that you read books that your child can understand.

- Choose books that show your child's interests.

Tell Me a Story

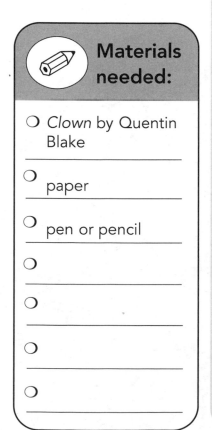

Purpose: To give the adult and child an opportunity to share a book

Process:

1. The adult and child go through the wordless picture book *Clown* together, making up the story as they go. (You can try creating similar activities with other books from the Recommended Books list.)

2. When they finish reading, they go back through the book and the adult writes down what the child thinks the characters would be saying if text were there. This can be done on regular notebook paper.

3. At the conclusion of this activity, the "Making a Family Book" take-home activity should be described for discussion the following week.

Materials needed:

○ *Clown* by Quentin Blake

○ paper

○ pen or pencil

○ _____

○ _____

○ _____

○ _____

Displaying a Sense of Audience

63

Displaying a Sense of Audience

TAKE-HOME ACTIVITY

Making a Family Book

 Purpose: To give the adult and child a chance to share stories involving family

Process:

1. Write a short story about your family.

2. Write about each person in your family as dictated by your child.

3. Have your child draw a picture of each person on his or her own page.

4. Draw a picture of the whole family on the cover of the folder.

5. Put the family pages in the folder to make your own family book.

Materials needed:

○ three-hole punched paper

○ blank paper

○ three-hole paper folder

○ crayons or markers

○ pen or pencil

○ _____

○ _____

○ _____

Recommended Books

The recommended books for this behavior were chosen because they give the adult and child an opportunity to talk. Some of the books are designed to teach the child. Other books can be used to encourage story sharing. All of the books encourage interaction between the adult and child.

Blake, Q. (1998). *Clown.* New York: Henry Holt.

A toy clown is out on his own trying to find a home. The clown does find some friends along his way in this wordless picture book.

Boynton, S. (1984). *Blue hat, green hat.* New York: Workman.

Teaching children colors is a focus of this book. Children are also introduced to different articles of clothing.

Coleman, E. (1999). *White socks only.* Morton Grove, IL: Albert Whitman.

Set years ago, a young African American girl goes to town. She is thirsty and goes to drink from a water fountain that reads "Whites only." She is wearing black shoes but white socks, so she takes off the shoes thinking this is what the sign means. Her action makes many others leap into action in this civil rights story.

Hanson, P. (2003). *My granny's purse.* New York: Workman.

This interactive book allows children to actually pull things out of Granny's purse. There are flaps to open, strings to untie, and spaces to look into. Easy to talk about with a child, this book is a purse full of fun.

Henkes, K. (1996). *Chrysanthemum.* New York: William Morrow.

Young Chrysanthemum likes her name until she gets to kindergarten. Her fellow students tease her, and she begins to think her name isn't so great. Fortunately, her parents are there to help her feel better about her name and ultimately about herself.

Promoting Interactive Reading and Supporting Comprehension

with Adam Severson

The strategies and accompanying activities in this section are designed to promote interactive reading and also provide ways to support comprehension. Being able to go beyond decoding to comprehending is essential for a child to become a successful reader. These activities provide beginning steps to help the adult guide the child toward understanding text. As in Chapter 4, puppets or people can be used to model the tips given at the beginning of the session.

BEHAVIORS IN CATEGORY II

BEHAVIOR 1: Posing and Soliciting Questions

BEHAVIOR 2: Identifying and Understanding Pictures and Words

BEHAVIOR 3: Relating Content to Personal Experiences

BEHAVIOR 4: Pausing to Answer Questions

BEHAVIOR

1

Posing and Soliciting Questions

- Adult poses and solicits questions about the book's content.

- Child responds to questions about the book.

PARENT/CAREGIVER TIPS FOR BEHAVIOR 1

- Ask your child questions when you get to things he or she may be curious about in the story.

- Ask your child about things he or she may recognize.

- Slow down your reading when you come to a part where your child might ask you a question.

- Be sure to stop and listen before answering when your child does ask you a question.

- Let questions lead to other questions.

Nine Magic Wishes

Purpose: To give children a chance to practice asking questions and adults an opportunity to encourage questioning by the child

Process:

1. The adult reads *9 Magic Wishes* aloud to the child. (You can try creating similar activities with other books from the Recommended Books list.)

2. As the book is being read, the adult stops at each wish to discuss with the child what is happening in the book.

3. The adult asks the child what thoughts he or she has about each wish in the book.

4. The child is given a chance to tell his or her thoughts after each wish and to ask the adult his or her thoughts, too.

5. After the pair has finished the book, they each come up with nine wishes for themselves and the adult writes them down to share with the group.

6. At the conclusion of this activity, the "Guess What?" take-home activity is described for discussion the following week.

Materials needed:

○ *9 Magic Wishes* by Shirley Jackson

○ paper

○ pen or pencil

○

○

○

Posing and Soliciting Questions

Guess What?

Purpose: To encourage discussion and questioning between the dyads

Process:

1. Draw a picture of something and have your child draw one, too.

2. Be sure you can't see each other's pictures.

3. After you both are done, play "Guess What?"

4. Without seeing each other's pictures, start trying to guess what your child drew, asking questions like "Is it a person?" "Is it red?"

5. After you have guessed the child's picture, switch roles with your child.

Materials needed:

○ paper

○ crayons or markers

○ _____

○ _____

○ _____

70

Posing and Soliciting Questions

Recommended Books

The books recommended for this behavior give the dyads multiple opportunities to ask questions. Children can easily generate questions from these stories.

Bruce, L. (2003). *Fran's friend.* **New York: Bloomsburg Children's Books.**

Fran has a dog named Fred. Fred wants to play, but Fran keeps shooing him away. Fred feels bad that Fran will not play with him, but Fran is making a surprise for him. Read and find out what the surprise is!

Denslow, S. (2000). *Big wolf and little wolf.* **New York: Greenwillow.**

A gray wolf father and son sing to each other one night. Suddenly, noises in the night startle them! Read and find out what is causing the noises.

Durant, A. (2000). *Big bad bunny.* **New York: Dutton's Children's Books.**

A big, bad bunny is looking for money. As he goes along, he takes whatever the other animals have since they don't have money. Finally, he gets to a bank, and a wise, old bunny teaches him a lesson. The big, bad bunny realizes he was wrong and makes a change for the better.

Hurd, T. (1985). *Mama don't allow.* **New York: HarperCollins.**

Miles gets a saxophone for his birthday. His parents don't want him playing inside so Miles and his swamp band practice elsewhere. One night they get a gig playing at a ball for a bunch of alligators. They have to use their brains and talents to avoid becoming the meal for the alligators.

Jackson, S. (2001). *9 magic wishes.* **New York: Farrar Straus Giroux.**

A little girl gets nine wishes from a magician who comes down her street. But she doesn't wish for money, fame, or anything else that most people would think of. Her wishes are a little bit different.

Munsch, R. (1992). *Purple, green, and yellow.* **Toronto: Annick Press.**

Young Brigid gets a little overzealous with her markers. She starts out just coloring a little. Soon, she's colored all over herself but has colored herself so well that she's a mess!

Rosen, M. (1997). *We're going on a bear hunt.* **New York: Simon & Schuster Children's.**

A father and his four children are heading out to find a bear. When they do, they have to run home to get away.

Shannon, D. (1998). *No, David!* **New York: Blue Sky Press.**

David moves from one bad behavior to the next in this book of simple words and colorful, vivid illustrations. This book is also available in Spanish as *¡No, David!*

71

BEHAVIOR 2

Identifying and Understanding Pictures and Words

- Adult points to pictures and words to assist the child in identification and understanding.

- Child responds to adult cues or identifies pictures and words on his or her own.

PARENT/CAREGIVER TIPS FOR BEHAVIOR 2

- Be sure to point to pictures, words, or letters that your child might recognize.

- Ask your child to tell you something about what is in the pictures.

- Look for simple words in the book that your child might know.

- Ask your child to say the word he or she knows to you.

- Each time a special repeated word appears in the story, you might stop and have the child read that word.

- Read your child's favorite books with him or her over and over to help your child recognize pictures and words.

Alphabet Book

Purpose:

To give the adult an opportunity to point out words and pictures to the child using the alphabet

Process:

1. Hand out the alphabet book materials.

2. The adult and child look through magazines and cut out pictures that start with different letters.

3. The adult and child paste pictures of objects and people that start with the same letter on pieces of construction paper and talk about the first letter of the objects or people on each page.

4. The adult or child writes the letter on the page. The adult or child also can write what the picture is (e.g., C is for corn).

5. Finally, the adult and child can make a cover and then tie all of the pages together with yarn to make a book.

6. At the conclusion of this activity, the "Riddles" take-home activity is discussed for the following week.

Materials needed:

○ hole-punched construction paper

○ magazines and newspapers

○ safety scissors

○ gluestick

○ crayons or markers

○ yarn

○ _____

○ _____

○ _____

Identifying and Understanding Pictures and Words

Identifying and Understanding Pictures and Words

Riddles

 Purpose:

Process:

To have the adult and child point to words and pictures in the book that the child knows or can learn

1. Read *Q is for Duck* to your child. (You can try creating similar activities with other books from the Recommended Books list.)

2. As you read the story, ask your child to try to guess the answers to the riddles.

3. If your child has trouble, ask questions or let him or her ask you questions that might help your child get the answer, calling attention to the alphabet letters and the objects that start with those letters.

4. Try having your child make up some alphabet riddles, and write them down to share with others (e.g., I am green, and I look like seaweed. What am I?).

Materials needed:

○ *Q is for Duck: An Alphabet Guessing Game* by Mary Elting

○ paper

○ pen or pencil

○

○

○

Recommended Books

The following books are ideal for pointing out words that children may know. Pictures in the books go with the words, and the child may be able to guess specific words using those pictures. Children have many opportunities to respond using these books.

Ada, F.A. (2001). *Gathering the sun: An alphabet in English and Spanish.* **New York: William Morrow.**

Gathering the Sun is a bilingual book that uses the everyday experiences of farm workers as the basis for simple poems, one for each letter of the Spanish alphabet.

Ayala, L., & Isona-Rodríguez, M. (1995). *Los Niños Alfabéticos.* **Watertown, MA: Charlesbridge.**

Poems for each letter of the Spanish alphabet and illustrations of children acting out the letters of the Spanish alphabet are part of this book available only in Spanish.

Bahan, B. (1994). *My ABC signs of animal friends.* **New York: Scholastic.**

Alec the alligator, Betty the bird, Conrad the cat, and so forth are the characters in this alphabet book that goes through animals that match the letters of the alphabet.

Calmenson, S. (1993). *It begins with an A.* **New York: Scholastic.**

This is an alphabet riddle book. Young readers will get to think about what is being described on each page.

Elting, M. (1985). *Q is for duck: An alphabet guessing game.* **Minneapolis: Sagebrush Education Resources.**

The reader gets to learn things about animals by using the alphabet throughout this book. However, the letters don't stand for what you think they might. For example, A is for zoo. Find out why!

Fisher, V. (2004). *Ellsworth's extraordinary electric ears: And other amazing alphabet anecdotes.* **New York: Atheneum.**

Each page in this unique alphabet book focuses on a specific letter and features an illustration of many items that begin with that letter. The text is both alliterative and amusing.

Martin, B., & Archambault, J. (2000). *Chicka chicka boom boom.* **New York: Simon & Schuster Children's.**

This alphabet book goes through the letters as if they were people. The letters all climb to the top of a coconut tree, but then all of the lowercase letters fall down—BOOM!

Miller, M. (1990). *Who uses this?* **New York: Scholastic.**

Margaret Miller has pictures of different objects in this book. The reader tries to figure out who might use what is pictured on the page.

Identifying and Understanding Pictures and Words

Pandell, K. (1996). *Animal action ABC.* **New York: Scholastic.**

This book has wonderful pictures taken of animals in the wild. Each page has a picture of a different animal doing a different action that connects to a letter of the alphabet.

Rose, D. (2000). *Into the a, b, sea.* **New York: Scholastic.**

With an alphabet of sea creatures, this book takes the reader where anemones sting, barnacles cling, crabs crawl in, and so forth. Different sea animals are shown in this alphabet book doing different things in the water.

Rurrs, M. (2001). *A Pacific alphabet.* **Toronto: Whitecap Books.**

Each page talks about different things beginning with the letters of the alphabet. Every page includes wonderful illustrations of happenings near or in the Pacific Ocean.

Sandved, K. (1996). *The butterfly alphabet.* **New York: Scholastic.**

This beautiful book shows letters of the alphabet on butterfly wings. The story goes along with the letters of the alphabet.

BEHAVIOR 3

Relating Content to Personal Experiences

- Adult relates the book's content and the child's responses to personal experiences.

- Child attempts to relate the book's content to personal experiences.

PARENT/CAREGIVER TIPS FOR BEHAVIOR 3

- Try to find things in the book that your child knows and talk about them.

- Be sure you give your child a chance to talk, and be sure you listen.

- If your child talks about something in the book that is a part of his or her everyday life, talk more about it.

- By pointing out something in a book that is familiar to a child, the child is more likely to pay attention and help read the story.

Relating Content to Personal Experiences

A Terrible, Horrible, No Good, Very Bad Day

Purpose: To give the dyads a book that they can read and discuss that relates to their lives

Process:

1. Read *Alexander and the Terrible, Horrible, No Good, Very Bad Day* aloud to the group. (You can try creating similar activities with other books from the Recommended Books list.)

2. Discuss the book and ask adults and children as a group to talk about some of their own terrible, horrible, no good, very bad days.

3. After the discussion, have each adult and child work together to write about or discuss a terrible, horrible, no good, very bad day that the child had.

4. The child can dictate the text of a story to the adult, and they can work together to draw pictures of what happened during that day.

Materials needed:

○ *Alexander and the Terrible, Horrible, No Good, Very Bad Day* by Judith Viorst

○ story paper

○ pen or pencil

○ crayons or markers

○

○

○

78

CLASS ACTIVITY

I Like It When . . .

Purpose: To facilitate discussion in the dyads about personal connections in the book and life experiences

Process:

1. Read *I Like It When.* (You can try creating similar activities with other books from the Recommended Books list.)

2. The adult has the child come up with three "I like it when…" sentences and writes them down.

3. The adult chooses the child's favorite "I like it when…" sentence, and the two of them draw a picture of it together.

4. The adult and child share the picture with others in the class.

5. At the conclusion of this activity, the "How We Grow" take-home activity could be described for discussion the following week.

Materials needed:

○ *I Like It When* by Mary Murphy

○ paper

○ pen or pencil

○ crayons or markers

○ _____

○ _____

○ _____

Relating Content to Personal Experiences

How We Grow

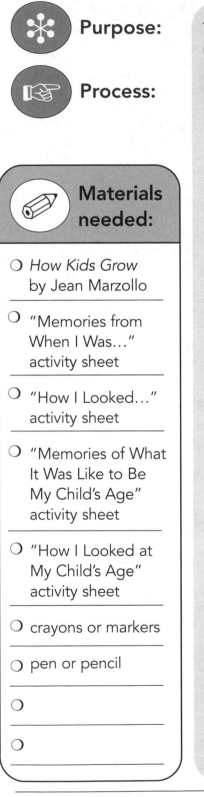

Purpose: To allow the adult and child an opportunity to practice making personal connections to books at home

Process:

1. Read *How Kids Grow* with your child. (You can try creating similar activities with other books from the Recommended Books list.)

2. Ask your child what he or she remembers about being a year younger, 2 years younger, and 3 years younger.

3. Have your child draw pictures of these memories on the "Memories from When I Was…" sheet that you were given.

4. Write what your child says on the back of this page.

5. Have your child draw you a picture of what he or she looked like 1, 2, and 3 years ago on the "How I Looked…" sheet you were given.

6. Tell your child about how you grew up and what is different now.

7. Draw a favorite memory of something you did when you were your child's age on the "Memories of What It Was Like to Be My Child's Age" sheet you were given.

8. Write this memory on the back of the page.

9. Have your child draw a picture of how he or she thinks you looked when you were his or her age on the "How I Looked at My Child's Age" sheet.

10. If you have pictures of your child through the years, look at them and talk about them with him or her.

11. Share your pictures with other family members.

Materials needed:

○ *How Kids Grow* by Jean Marzollo

○ "Memories from When I Was…" activity sheet

○ "How I Looked…" activity sheet

○ "Memories of What It Was Like to Be My Child's Age" activity sheet

○ "How I Looked at My Child's Age" activity sheet

○ crayons or markers

○ pen or pencil

○ _____

○ _____

Relating Content to Personal Experiences

Memories from When I Was 3 Years Younger

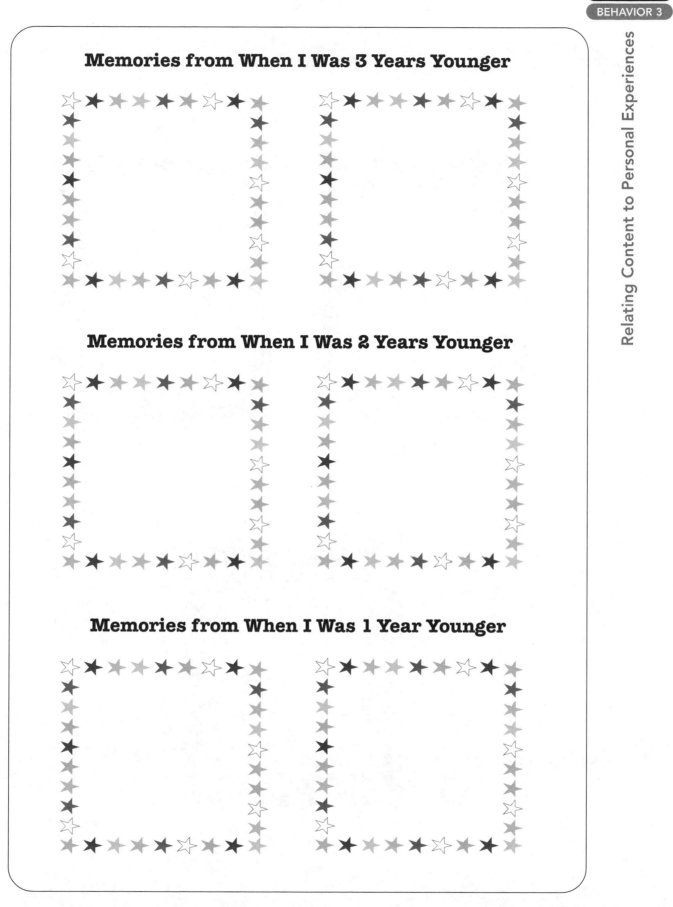

Memories from When I Was 2 Years Younger

Memories from When I Was 1 Year Younger

Relating Content to Personal Experiences

How I Looked . . .

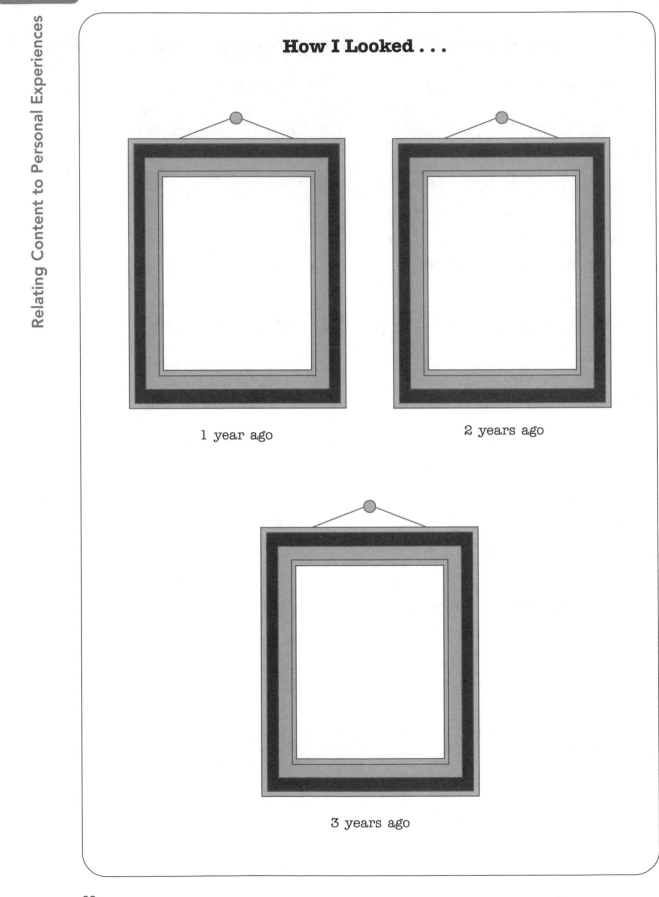

1 year ago

2 years ago

3 years ago

Memories of What It Was
Like to Be My Child's Age

Relating Content to Personal Experiences

Relating Content to Personal Experiences

**How I Looked
at My Child's Age**

Recommended Books

The following books were chosen because adults and children alike can make personal connections to the books. This gives the pairs an opportunity to talk about their connections.

Carlson, N. (1990). *I like me!* **New York: Puffin.**

This pig loves many of the things about herself. Find out why she likes herself and how she stays her best. This book is also available in Spanish as *Me Gusto Como Soy!*

Curtis, J.L. (1999). *When I was little: A four-year old's memoir of her youth.* **New York: HarperFestival.**

As the 4-year-old narrator describes the story of her life events so far, readers can explore the items in the detailed drawings while having their funny bones tickled. This book is also available in Spanish as *Cuando Yo Ere Pequeña: Memorías De Una Niña De Cuatro Anos.*

Fleming, D. (1992). *Lunch.* **New York: Scholastic.**

A very hungry mouse starts eating everything he sees for his lunch. Apples, peas, grapes, watermelons, and much more! By the time he's done, it is...dinnertime!

Garza, C.L. (2000). *In my family/En mi familia.* **San Francisco: Children's Book Press.**

The author describes in simple words and beautiful pictures her memories of growing up in a traditional Mexican American community in Texas. Written in English and Spanish.

Morris, A. (1994). *Loving.* **New York: Scholastic.**

All over the world, people may look different, eat different foods, and play different games, but love for others is often shown in the same sorts of ways.

Morzollo, J. (1998). *How kids grow.* **New York: Scholastic.**

As people grow up, they can do different things at different ages. This book shows how children grow and what they can do at what ages.

Murphy, M. (1997). *I like it when....* **San Diego: Harcourt.**

A young penguin likes many things. Eating, dancing, and holding hands are just some of the things this penguin enjoys doing when spending time with the older penguin.

Viorst, J. (1972). *Alexander and the terrible, horrible, no good, very bad day.* **New York: Simon & Schuster Children's.**

Alexander's day does not start out well as he finds gum in his hair when he wakes up. As the day goes on, things progressively get worse. A great book to read to a child who has had a bad day.

Willems, M. (2004). *Knuffle bunny: A cautionary tale.* **New York: Hyperion.**

While on an errand to do laundry with her dad, little Trixie misplaces her well-loved stuffed bunny and tries in vain to let her dad know. He misunderstands her gibberish at every turn in this amusing lost-and-found tale.

BEHAVIOR

4

Pausing to Answer Questions

- Adult pauses to answer questions that the child poses.

- Child poses questions about the story and related topics.

PARENT/CAREGIVER TIPS FOR BEHAVIOR 4

- Ask your child questions when you get to things that he or she may be curious about in the story.

- Ask your child questions about things that he or she may recognize.

- Slow down your reading when there seems to be a part that may lead your child to ask you questions.

- Be sure to stop and listen before answering when your child does ask you a question.

- When your child asks you questions, be sure you take time to understand what he or she is asking.

- One question can lead to many others, which is a good thing. It lets you and your child enjoy the book and learn together.

- Do not be afraid to tell your child when you do not know an answer.

- Look up any answers to questions that you do not know when you can.

CLASS ACTIVITY

Animal Poetry

Purpose: To give the adult an opportunity to ask questions and practice pausing to listen to the child and to allow the child to ask questions on his or her own

Process:

1. The child picks an animal.

2. The adult asks the child for characteristics of the animal, and fills them in on the "A Poem About an Animal" to make a pattern poem.

3. After the poem is done, the adult reads it to the child. The child draws a picture on the back of the poem sheet based on the characteristics. He or she can ask the adult questions about things that he or she may have forgotten.

4. Use the other poem sheets: "A Poem About Me," "A Poem About My Family," and "A Poem from My Imagination." They can be used in class or sent home as take-home activities. Instructions for these pattern poems are as follows:

A Poem About Me and A Poem About My Family

Ask your child the information printed above each line on the poetry sheet, and fill in the blank below it (e.g., child's first name: Emily).

A Poem from My Imagination

- Ask your child to use his or her imagination to think of something or someone.

- Start by writing the title.

- Ask your child questions to help him or her to generate ideas.

- Use the answers to the questions to help your child create this pattern poem.

Materials needed:

○ "A Poem About an Animal" activity sheet

○ "A Poem About Me" activity sheet

○ "A Poem About My Family" activity sheet

○ "A Poem from My Imagination" activity sheet

○ pen or pencil

○ crayons or markers

○ paper

○

○

○

87

A Poem About an Animal

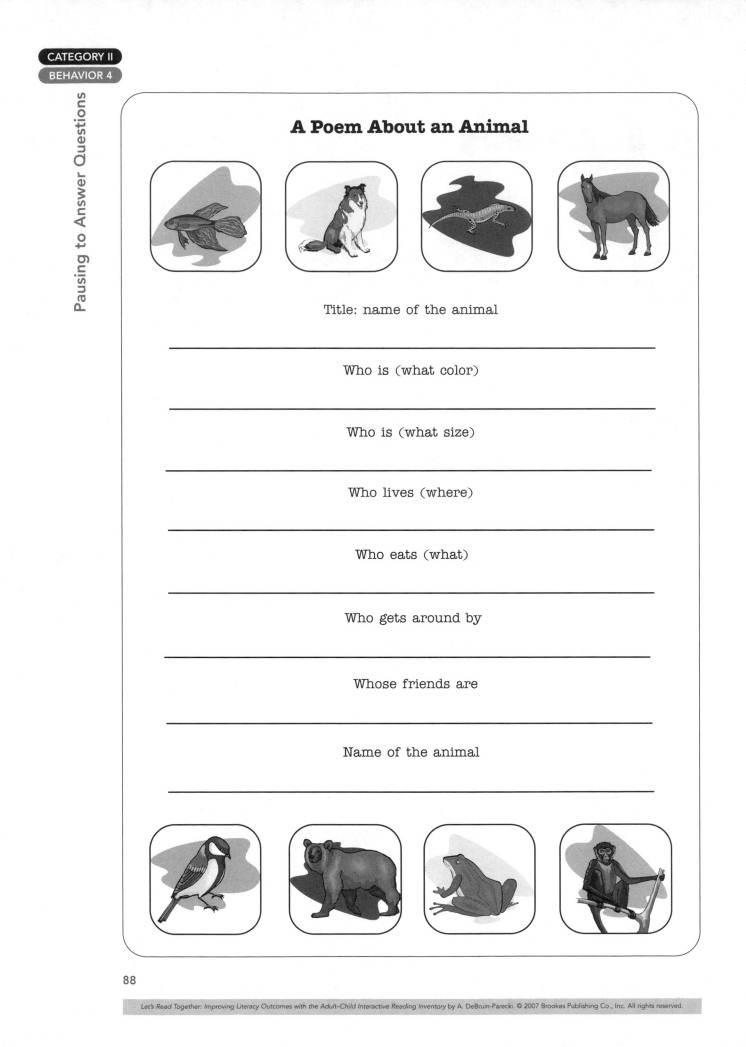

Title: name of the animal

_____

Who is (what color)

_____

Who is (what size)

_____

Who lives (where)

_____

Who eats (what)

_____

Who gets around by

_____

Whose friends are

_____

Name of the animal

_____

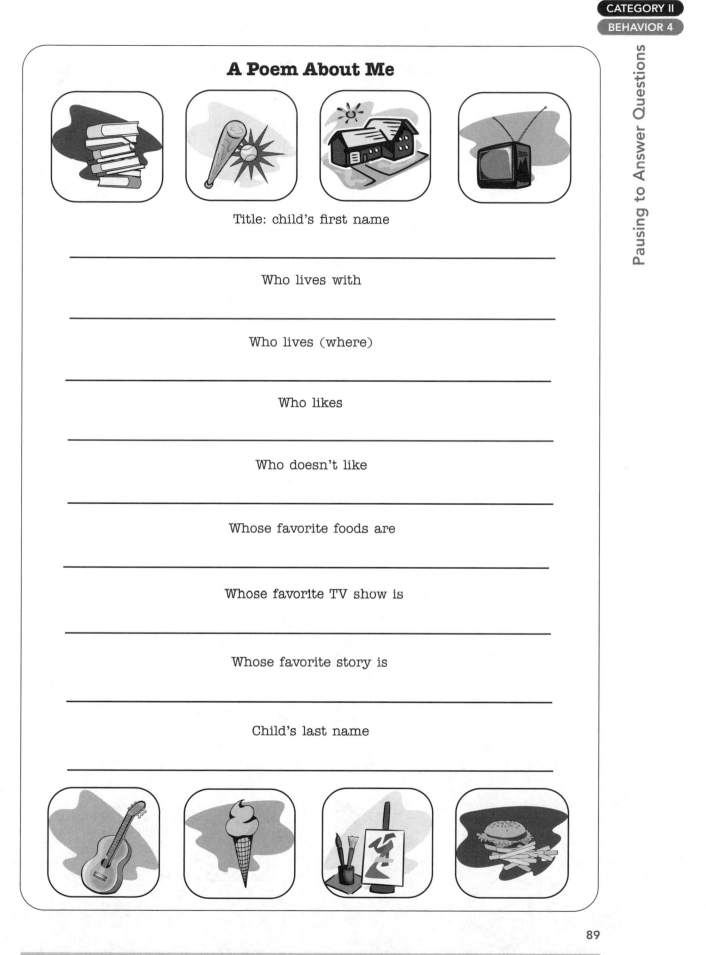

A Poem About Me

Title: child's first name

_____

Who lives with

_____

Who lives (where)

_____

Who likes

_____

Who doesn't like

_____

Whose favorite foods are

_____

Whose favorite TV show is

_____

Whose favorite story is

_____

Child's last name

_____

89

Pausing to Answer Questions

A Poem About My Family

Title: my family

_____

Names of people in my family

_____

Who likes to (do things together)

_____

Who goes together (where)

_____

Who all like to play these games together

_____

Whose favorite holiday is

_____

Whose favorite movie is

_____

Who reads with me

_____

My name

_____

90

A Poem from My Imagination

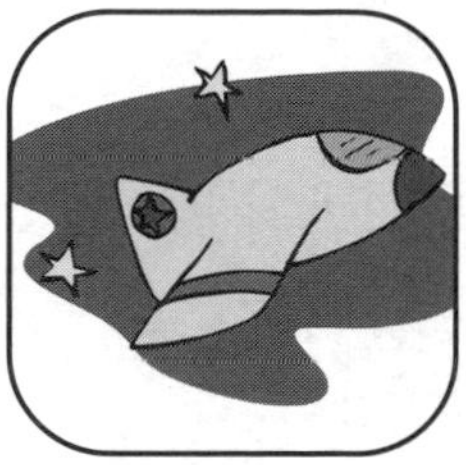

Make up your own poem

Title:

_____

_____

_____

_____

_____

_____

_____

Pausing to Answer Questions

Mama, Do You Love Me?

Purpose: To give the adult practice pausing to ask and answer questions, and to give the child an opportunity to ask questions

Process:

1. Read *Mama, Do You Love Me?* to your child. (You can try creating similar activities with other books from the Recommended Books list.)

2. Each time the child in the story asks a question, ask your child what he or she thinks the Mama will say.

3. When you finish reading the story, make up a story with your child. Read each question on the "A Sunny Day" activity sheet and write down your child's answer to each question on the lines provided. Have your child draw a picture in the box next to the written answer.

4. Using the answers to the questions and the child's pictures, retell the story together.

5. You can play a similar question game with your child using other books or by making up a story that is similar to this one.

Materials needed:

○ *Mama, Do You Love Me?* by Barbara Joose

○ "A Sunny Day" activity sheet

○ paper

○ pen or pencil

○ crayons or markers

○ _____

○ _____

○ _____

A Sunny Day: A Story
Filled with Questions

1. Where can we go on a
   sunny day?

   _____

   _____

   _____

2. What would you wear?

   _____

   _____

   _____

3. What is your favorite thing to
   do there?

   _____

   _____

   _____

Pausing to Answer Questions

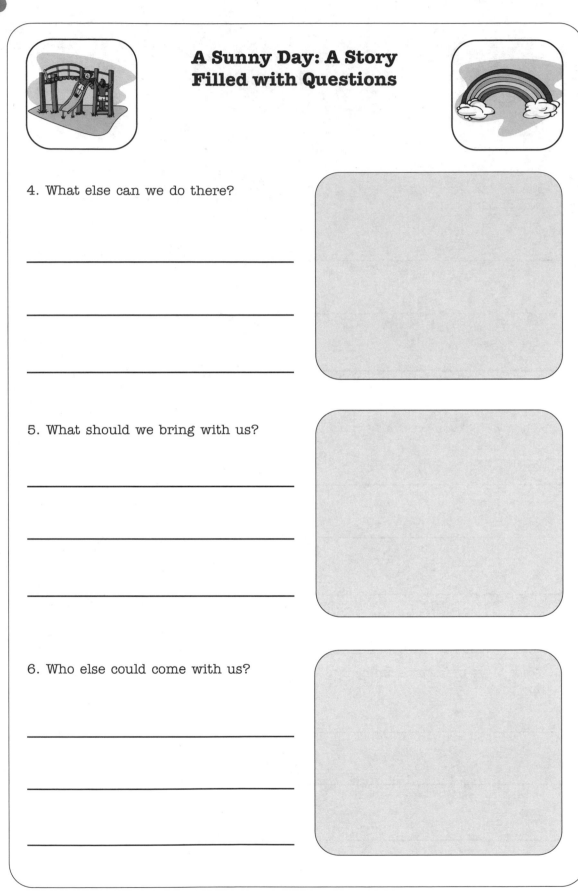

A Sunny Day: A Story Filled with Questions

4. What else can we do there?

_____

_____

_____

5. What should we bring with us?

_____

_____

_____

6. Who else could come with us?

_____

_____

_____

A Sunny Day: A Story
Filled with Questions

7. What can we do together?

_____

_____

_____

8. How would we know when it is time to go home?

_____

_____

_____

Recommended Books

These books are wonderful for questioning. Adults and children both have numerous opportunities to ask questions. The adults also get an opportunity to pause and answer the questions children pose. These books promote questioning on the part of children in particular.

Asch, F. (1982). *Happy birthday, Moon.* **New York: Scholastic.**

A bear wants to give the moon a birthday present, so he has a chat with the moon and ends up buying the moon a hat. Then the moon shows its generosity.

Cuyler, M. (1993). *That's good! That's bad!* **New York: Henry Holt and Company.**

A boy gets into all sorts of adventures with animals. First, a balloon takes him up in the air. That's good, but then it pops. That's bad. This story takes the boy through an adventure but eventually back to his parents.

Joose, B. (1998). *Mama, do you love me?* **San Francisco: Chronicle Books.**

Set in the Arctic, a mother tells of her unconditional love for her child. Her child asks many questions about her mother's love for her. The mother reassures her child throughout the story that she loves her daughter no matter what. This book is also available in Spanish as *¿Me Quieres, Mamá?*

Lionni, L. (1967). *Frederick.* **New York: Dragonfly Books.**

All of the other mice are hard at work getting ready for winter. Frederick is off in his own little dreamland and looking lazy. But Frederick does contribute something during the winter: his poetry.

Martin, B. (1991). *Polar bear, polar bear, what do you hear?* **New York: Henry Holt and Company.**

The polar bear hears many things. Lions roaring and hippos snorting are just a couple of things this polar bear hears. Illustrated by Eric Carle, the pictures in this book are amazing. This book is also available in Spanish as *Oso Polar, Oso Polar, ¿Qué es Ese Ruido?*

Noble, T. (1980). *The day Jimmy's boa ate the wash.* **New York: Scholastic.**

The class is on a normal field trip to a farm. Things aren't normal for long. Jimmy pulls out his boa constrictor to meet the other animals.

Using Literacy Strategies

with Adam Severson

The strategies in this section are designed to help children understand and make sense of stories. Adults are encouraged to use these strategies to aid children in their development of comprehension and vocabulary skills. These strategies allow the adult to work with the child to promote the child's use of these strategies independently. This will eventually help the child to construct meaning from text with little or no adult assistance.

BEHAVIORS IN CATEGORY III

BEHAVIOR 1: Identifying Visual Cues

BEHAVIOR 2: Predicting What Happens Next

BEHAVIOR 3: Recalling Information

BEHAVIOR 4: Elaborating on Ideas

Identifying Visual Cues

BEHAVIOR
1

Identifying Visual Cues

- Adult identifies visual cues related to story reading (e.g., pictures, repetitive words).

- Child responds to the adult and/or identifies visual cues related to the story.

PARENT/CAREGIVER TIPS FOR BEHAVIOR 1

- Take time before you read the story to look through the book so you will be able to point out often-used pictures or words.

- Be sure to point to pictures or words your child might know.

- Begin to match spoken words to written words and point out letter–sound matches.

- Keep your child interested by pointing out and having him or her identify letters and words that help him or her tell the story.

- Each time a repeated word appears in the story, you might stop and have the child read that word.

- Try to give your child a chance to find pictures or words before you read the page.

CLASS ACTIVITY

Rebus Poems

Purpose: To practice using visual cues, such as words and pictures, to aid in comprehension

Process:

1. The teacher reads *I Love You: A Rebus Poem* aloud, making sure to point out the pictures that are part of the text to show the rebus focus of the book. The rebus focus involves pictures inserted in the place of certain words to help children begin to read.

2. Using the activity sheet, the adult and child will make up a rebus poem. It does not have to rhyme. The child should draw a picture to represent a word as often as possible.

3. The adult and child should read the poem together.

4. Members of the class will pass the poems around the room, reading other classmates' poems.

5. At the conclusion of this activity, the "Repeated Words" take-home activity sheet could be sent home for discussion the following week.

Materials needed:

○ *I Love You: A Rebus Poem* by Jean Marzollo

○ "Rebus Poem" activity sheet

○ pen or pencil

○ crayons or markers

○ _____

○ _____

○ _____

99

Identifying Visual Cues

Rebus Poem

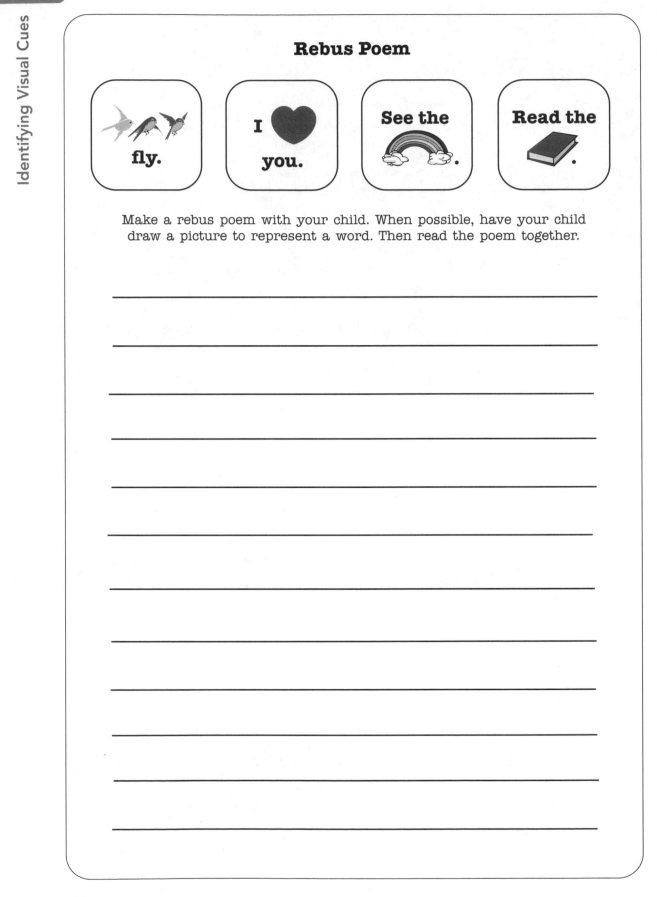

fly.

I ♥ you.

See the 🌈.

Read the 📕.

Make a rebus poem with your child. When possible, have your child draw a picture to represent a word. Then read the poem together.

_____

_____

_____

_____

_____

_____

_____

_____

_____

TAKE-HOME ACTIVITY

Using Repeated Words

Purpose:

Process:

To assist the child in recognizing and indentifying repeated words and phrases in a story or poem

1. Read the book *Miss Mary Mack* aloud to your child.

2. As you read, see if your child can begin to fill in the repeated words before you say them.

3. Another way to enjoy this book is to sing the song with your child or play a clapping game.

4. What other rhyming songs do you know that use repeated words? Try teaching your child some of them (e.g., "Mama Don't Allow"). The following rhymes are examples of repeating words:

> I spy a cat, cat, cat,
> And a tall top hat, hat, hat,
> And a little green lizard, lizard, lizard
> Upon the mat, mat, mat.

> As I was going along, long, long,
> A-singing a comical song, song, song,
> The lane that I went was so long, long, long,
> And the song that I sung was so long, long, long,
> And so I went singing along.

> To market, to market, to buy a fat pig.
> Home again, home again, jiggety jig.
> To market, to market, to buy a fat hog.
> Home again, home again, jiggety jog.
> To market, to market, to buy a plum bun.
> Home again, home again, market is done.

5. Can you write a song, poem, or clapping game together that uses repeated words? Practice writing your song, poem, or clapping game.

6. Once you've completed your song, poem, or clapping game, write it on the take-home activity sheet and draw pictures to go with it. Then, practice saying your song, poem, or clapping game.

7. The song, poem, or clapping game will be collected for a class book the following week.

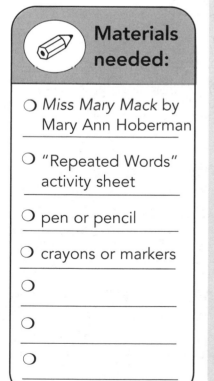

Materials needed:

○ *Miss Mary Mack* by Mary Ann Hoberman

○ "Repeated Words" activity sheet

○ pen or pencil

○ crayons or markers

○

○

○

101

Identifying Visual Cues

Repeated Words

Mr. Marty
moose
moose
moose

Sing
La di da di
day
La di da di
day

Write a song, poem, or clapping game
together that uses repeated words.

_____

_____

_____

_____

_____

_____

_____

_____

_____

102

Recommended Books

The following books are full of visual cues that aid in the storytelling. They give the adult and child an opportunity to practice using visual cues related to meaning. Visual cues are very evident throughout these books.

Bergman, M. (2005). *Snip snap! What's that?* **New York: Greenwillow.**

A big alligator sneaks up the stairs and chases after three children. Are the children scared? You bet they are! After a while, they can't take anymore and decide to tell the alligator how they feel.

Chorao, K. (1999). *Knock at the door.* **New York: Scholastic.**

This Little Piggy and Pat-a-cake are among other cute rhymes for children. Check out this book with 20 different rhymes!

Cronin, D. (2000). *Click, clack, moo: Cows that type.* **New York: Simon & Schuster.**

Farmer Brown starts to hear strange things in his barn. His very intelligent cows are tired of their working conditions, so they begin leaving him notes and bargaining for things. The next thing Farmer Brown knows, other animals have sided with the cows and a strike is planned. This book is also available in Spanish as *Clic, Clac, Muu: Vacas Escritotias.*

Hoberman, M.A., & Westcott, N.B. (1998). Miss Mary Mack. New York: Little Brown & Co.

This book presents a popular children's hand-clapping game complete with colorful illustrations and musical notations.

Hurd, T. (1985). *Mama don't allow.* **New York: HarperCollins.**

Lyrics of the song, "Mama Don't Allow," are presented along with an animal story complete with jazzy pictures and musical notation.

Lionni, L. (1975). *A color of his own.* **New York: Scholastic.**

Other animals, like parrots and goldfish, have colors of their own. What color is the chameleon going to be?

Marzollo, J. (2000). *I love you: A rebus poem.* **New York: Scholastic.**

Everyone loves a.... Each page of this book begins with those words, and then the picture shows what everyone loves.

Orozco, J.L. (1997). *Diez deditos and other play rhymes and action songs from Latin America.* **New York: Dutton Books.**

Lyrics to these songs and poems are presented in both English and Spanish along with easy-to-follow musical accompaniment and diagrams for the corresponding actions. The many poems and songs have repeated words, and teachers/parents have ample opportunities to get kids to participate.

Parker, V. (1996). *Bearobics.* **New York: Scholastic.**

Deep in the forest, there's a thumping, bumping sound, a drumming and a humming. What is going on? It's Bearobics! Read this hip-hop counting story.

Predicting What Happens Next

BEHAVIOR 2

Predicting What Happens Next

- Adult solicits predictions.
- Child is able to guess what will happen next based on picture cues.

PARENT/CAREGIVER TIPS FOR BEHAVIOR 2

- Help your child look for clues in the story that tell what will happen later in the book.

- Ask your child what will happen next in the story.

- Ask your child to explain his or her predictions.

- Allow your child a chance to look at the pictures and to think about what will happen in the story before you turn a page.

- Give your child a chance to talk about the story. Talk talk more about what your child has to say to find out what he might be thinking.

CLASS ACTIVITY

What Might Happen Next?

Purpose: To encourage the child to practice making predictions by having the adult use appropriate and timely prompts

Process:

1. Each adult and child are given 3 of the 12 activity sheets. Mix them up so that each dyad has different combinations.

2. The adult and child will talk about what they think will happen next on the basis of the picture.

3. The adult will then write down his or her and the child's ideas under the picture.

4. After each adult and child is done, ideas and pictures will be shared.

Materials needed:

○ 12 "What Do You Think is Going to Happen?" activity sheets

○ pen or pencil

○ _____

○ _____

○ _____

105

Predicting What Happens Next

What do you think is going to happen?
Why do you think that will happen?

_____

_____

_____

_____

_____

_____

_____

What do you think is going to happen?
Why do you think that will happen?

_____

_____

_____

_____

_____

_____

_____

Predicting What Happens Next

What do you think is going to happen?
Why do you think that will happen?

_____

_____

_____

_____

_____

_____

_____

What do you think is going to happen?
Why do you think that will happen?

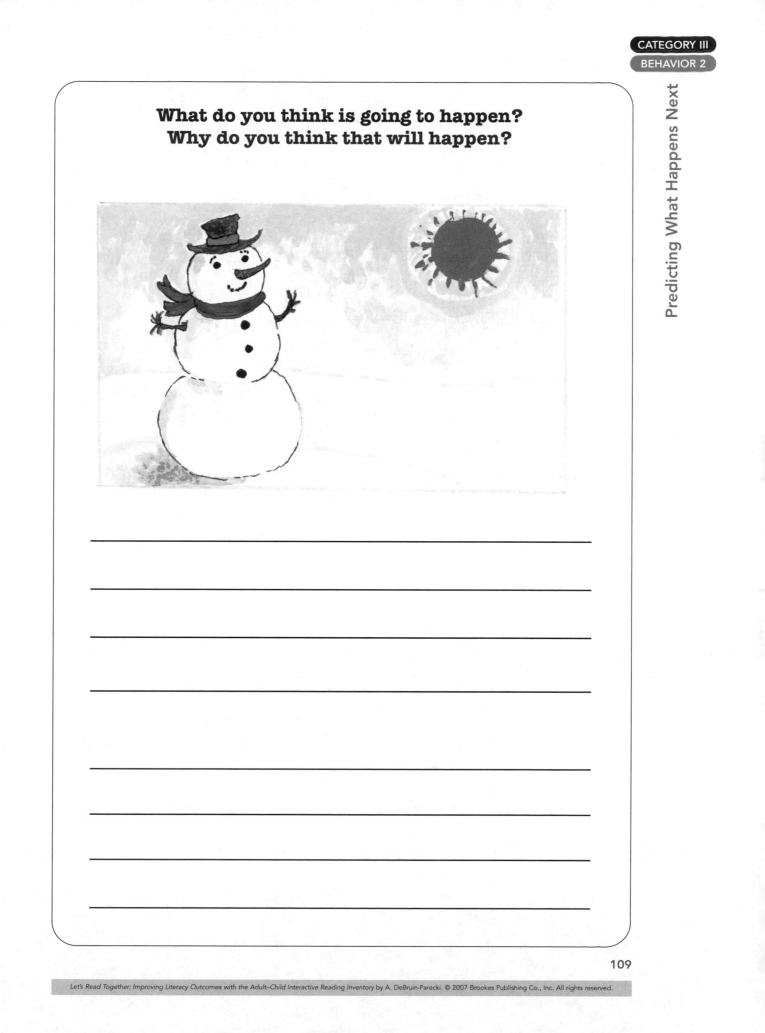

_____

_____

_____

_____

_____

_____

_____

Predicting What Happens Next

What do you think is going to happen?
Why do you think that will happen?

_____

_____

_____

_____

_____

_____

_____

What do you think is going to happen?
Why do you think that will happen?

_____

_____

_____

_____

_____

_____

_____

111

Predicting What Happens Next

What do you think is going to happen?
Why do you think that will happen?

_____

_____

_____

_____

_____

_____

What do you think is going to happen?
Why do you think that will happen?

_____

_____

_____

_____

_____

_____

_____

What do you think is going to happen?
Why do you think that will happen?

_____

_____

_____

_____

_____

_____

What do you think is going to happen?
Why do you think that will happen?

_____

_____

_____

_____

_____

_____

_____

What do you think is going to happen?
Why do you think that will happen?

_____

_____

_____

_____

_____

_____

_____

What do you think is going to happen?
Why do you think that will happen?

_____

_____

_____

_____

_____

_____

_____

Predicting What Happens Next

CLASS ACTIVITY

Picture Walk Predictions

✳ Purpose: To give the adult and child an opportunity to practice making predictions

☞ Process:

1. Explain and demonstrate a picture walk to the class. A picture walk is "reading" the book using the pictures and not reading the words.

2. Have the adult and child take a picture walk through *The Very Hungry Caterpillar*, stopping so the adult can ask the child for predictions.

3. Ask the adult to write down the child's predictions on the "Predicting the Story" activity sheet based on the pictures.

4. The adult will read the book to the child.

5. After the book has been read, the adult and child will look back at the predictions and draw a star next to the predictions that followed the story.

6. The adult can then help the child write down a two- or three-sentence reaction to the story.

7. At the conclusion of this activity, the "If You Give a Mouse a Cookie" activity sheet could be sent home for discussion the following week.

✎ Materials needed:

○ *The Very Hungry Caterpillar* by Eric Carle

○ "Predicting the Story" activity sheet

○ pen or pencil

○ _____

○ _____

○ _____

118

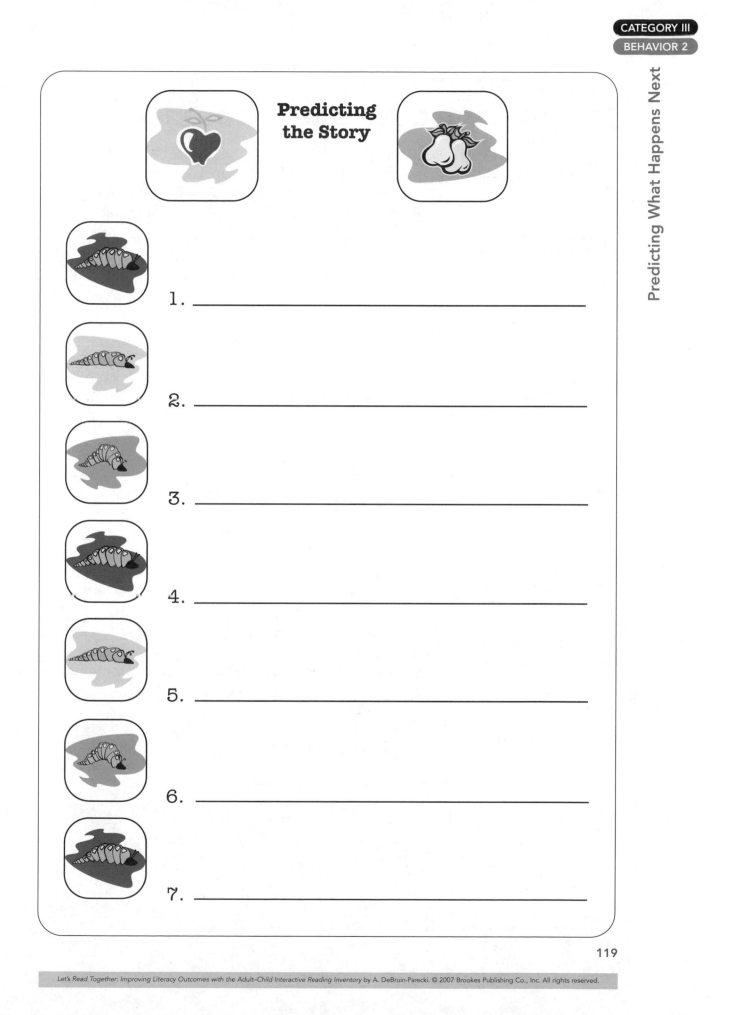

**Predicting
the Story**

1. _____

2. _____

3. _____

4. _____

5. _____

6. _____

7. _____

Predicting What Happens Next

If You Give a Mouse a Cookie

 **Purpose:** To promote adult and child interaction; to promote predictions—in this case, what the cookies will look like and taste like after the mix has been made

 **Process:**

1. Read *If You Give a Mouse a Cookie* to your child. (You can try creating similar activities with other books from the Recommended Books list.)

2. It's time to bake cookies with your child!

3. On the "Baking Cookies with Your Child" activity sheet, draw a picture of what your child thinks the cookies will look like and write what he or she thinks they will taste like.

4. The directions for making these cookies are on the activity sheet. (Use Nestle's Toll House Cookie Mix in a pouch; using ready-made or slice-it-yourself cookie dough doesn't provide enough time for interaction, which is one of the main reasons for doing this activity. If there are children who can't eat cookies, then read *If You Give a Pig a Pancake* instead and use a pancake mix.)

5. Please let your child help you measure the needed amounts of ingredients.

6. Let your child stir and help drop the cookies on the cookie sheet.

7. When the cookies are cooled, enjoy!

8. Look at the picture, and read your child's predictions. Ask your child if he or she was right.

Materials needed:

○ *If You Give a Mouse a Cookie* by Laura Numeroff

○ "Baking Cookies with Your Child" activity sheet

○ cookie mix, bowl, mixing spoon, liquid measuring cup, baking sheet, margarine, water

○ crayons or markers

○ pen or pencil

○ oven

○ _____

○ _____

120

Baking Cookies with Your Child

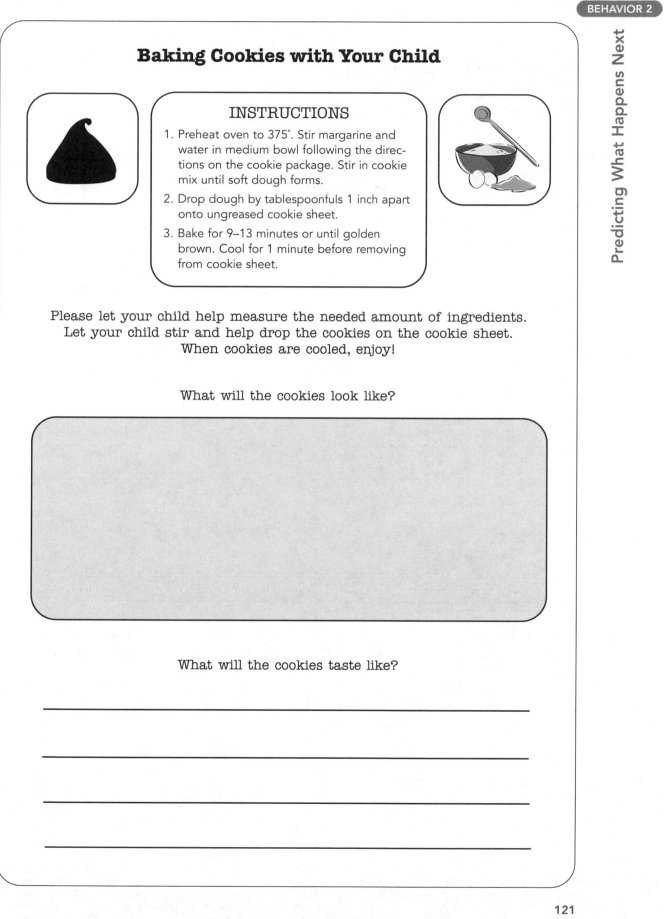

INSTRUCTIONS

1. Preheat oven to 375°. Stir margarine and water in medium bowl following the directions on the cookie package. Stir in cookie mix until soft dough forms.

2. Drop dough by tablespoonfuls 1 inch apart onto ungreased cookie sheet.

3. Bake for 9–13 minutes or until golden brown. Cool for 1 minute before removing from cookie sheet.

Please let your child help measure the needed amount of ingredients.
Let your child stir and help drop the cookies on the cookie sheet.
When cookies are cooled, enjoy!

What will the cookies look like?

What will the cookies taste like?

121

Predicting What Happens Next

Can You Predict What Will Happen?

 Purpose: To allow the adult and child an opportunity to practice predictions

Process:

1. Fill in the blanks on the activity sheet with your predictions.

2. Talk about why you think your predictions might be true.

Materials needed:

○ "If You Give Someone You Love a Hug…" activity sheet

○ pen or pencil

○ _____

○ _____

○ _____

If you give someone you love a hug . . .

That special person might feel . . .

_____

That special person might want to . . .

_____

And . . .

_____

And . . .

_____

And you might want to . . .

_____

If your child gives you a hug . . .

Your child might feel . . .

_____

Your child might want to . . .

_____

And . . .

_____

And . . .

_____

And you might want to . . .

_____

123

Recommended Books

Opportunities for predictions are obvious and prevalent throughout these books. The adult and child have multiple chances to talk and discuss predictions. This aids in improving children's comprehension.

Carle, E. (1986). *The very hungry caterpillar.* **New York: Putnam.**

A caterpillar hatches out of his egg and is very hungry. On the first day, he eats through one piece of food. The next day, he eats through two pieces. As the book continues, the caterpillar keeps eating until he turns into…a butterfly! This book is also available in Spanish as *La Oruga Muy Hambrienta.*

Christian, C. (1996). *Where's the baby?* **New York: Star Bright.**

The baby's toys are there, but where is the baby? Looking through the book, you can find the baby.

Fox, M. (1996). *Zoo-looking.* **New York: Mondo.**

Flora goes to the zoo to see the animals, but the animals like seeing her, too! She visits snakes, monkeys, and other creatures. The rhyming in the story makes this a fun book to read with your child.

Numeroff, L. (1985). *If you give a mouse a cookie.* **New York: HarperCollins.**

What happens if you give a mouse a cookie? He'll need a glass of milk to wash it down. As the mouse is given one thing, he needs something else. This book is also available in Spanish as *Si le Das Una Galletita a Un Ratón.*

Numeroff, L. (1998). *If you give a pig a pancake.* **New York: HarperCollins.**

If you give a pig a pancake, be ready to give him something to go with it. If a pig needs one thing, he also needs something else. This book is also available in Spanish as *Si le Das Un Panqueque a Una Cerdita.*

Tafuri, N. (1996). *Have you seen my duckling?* **New York: Greenwillow.**

A duckling is missing! Mother Duck looks all over the pond with her other ducklings following her. But no one else on the pond has seen her little duckling. Where is the duck? It's not as lost as you may think.

Willems, M. (2005). *Leonardo, the terrible monster.* **New York: Hyperion.**

Leonardo can't scare anyone. Then he finds Sam and is sure he can scare the tuna fish salad out of him. But when he meets Sam, he has a sudden change of heart and the two become best friends.

Williams, S. (1996). *I went walking.* **New York: Harcourt.**

A young child goes for a walk and meets many friendly animals. These animals look familiar and are many different colors. Read to find out what animals the child sees.

<table>
<tr><td>BEHAVIOR
3</td></tr>
</table>

Recalling Information

- Adult asks the child to recall information from the story.
- Child is able to recall information from the story.

PARENT/CAREGIVER TIPS FOR BEHAVIOR 3

- As you read the story, stop once in a while to ask your child to tell you what has happened so far.

- If your child can't remember, let your child use pictures to tell you what the story is about.

- Try to help your child to recall the events of the story in order.

- When you are done reading, have your child tell you the whole story.

Recalling Information

CLASS ACTIVITY

Story Map

Purpose: To understand what the child recalls after being read a story

Process:

1. The teacher explains the concept of a story map to the class and models the story map activity by asking a child to help.

2. The class reviews the questions on the "Story Map" activity sheet before starting the activity.

3. The adult reads *Goodnight, Moon,* or his or her child's favorite children's book, keeping the story map questions in mind.

4. When the adult finishes the story, he or she asks the child to recall information from the story following the order of the story map and has the child draw his or her ideas in the box that answers that question.

5. On the second story map sheet, the adult writes in each box what his or her child drew.

6. Using the two story map sheets, the adult and child retell the story together.

7. Discuss the "Is Your Mama a Llama?" take-home activity, and provide each of the dyads with three hole-punched llama head activity sheets.

Materials needed:

○ *Goodnight, Moon* by Margaret Wise Brown

○ "Story Map" activity sheet

○ pen or pencil

○ crayons or markers

○ _____

○ _____

○ _____

Story Map

Who was in the story?	Where did the story take place?
What happened at the beginning of the story?	What happened in the middle of the story?
What happened at the end of the story?	What did you think of the story?

Recalling Information

Is Your Mama a Llama?

Purpose: To give the child an opportunity to demonstrate what he or she recalls from the story and to provide the adult with information on what the child remembered

Process:

1. Read *Is Your Mama a Llama?* to your child. (You can try creating similar activities with other books from the Recommended Books list.)

2. As you read the book, ask the question, "Is your mama a llama?" After asking the question a couple of times, pause the next time to see if your child will ask the question.

3. Tell your child what a few of the animals are, and ask your child if he or she can then name others.

4. Take out the three llama activity sheets.

5. Have your child color the first llama head.

6. On the second llama head, have your child draw one of the things the llama was thinking in the story.

7. On the third llama head, write what the child drew in the llama's head on the lines provided.

8. Tie the sheets together with the string to make a mini book.

9. Bring the mini book to class so your child can share something he or she thought was in the llama's head.

Materials needed:

O *Is Your Mama a Llama?* by Deborah Guarino

O three hole-punched llama activity sheets

O pen or pencil

O crayons or markers

O string

O _____

O _____

O _____

_____

_____

_____

129

Recommended Books

The books recommended are written in a clear sequential manner. These books are excellent resources that help to determine how much a child can recall from a story.

Brown, M.W. (1991). *Goodnight, Moon.* **New York: HarperCollins.**

A rabbit is going to bed. As the sky gets darker, the rabbit says goodnight to each item in his room. This book is also available in Spanish as *Buenas Noches, Luna.*

Carlstrom, N. (1996). *Jesse Bear, what will you wear?* **New York: Simon & Schuster.**

This rhyming picture book follows Jesse Bear and what he decides to wear as he goes through his day. The rhymes are great for children to hear and recite.

Cook, S. (2004). *Good Night Pillow Fight.* **New York: HarperCollins.**

Putting a child to sleep can be difficult. It is even more difficult when the child rhymes what you say when you want him or her to sleep. It's time to lay down the law.

Curtis, J. (2000). *Where do balloons go?* **New York: HarperCollins.**

A little boy loses his balloon. Where does it go? He imagines the adventure that the balloon must take.

Freeman, D. (2005). *Earl the squirrel.* **New York: Viking.**

Earl's mother thinks it is time for Earl to find acorns on his own. He discovers an interesting way to do this.

Guarino, D. (1997). *Is your mama a llama?* **New York: Scholastic.**

A young llama tries to find out if his friends' mothers are llamas. The rhyming story shows how the llama finds out other animals have mothers that are like each of them. This book is also available in Spanish as *¿Tu Mamá es Una Llama?*

Madonna. (2004). *Yakov and the seven thieves.* **New York: Callaway Editions.**

Set in the Ukraine, this story is about Yakov. He wants a wise man to cure his son, who is very sick. The wise man cannot help him, but some unlikely people are able to help the ill son.

Senisi, E.B. (2002). *All kinds of friends, even green!* **Bethesda, MD: Woodbine House.**

A young boy with spina bifida finds a special friend, a green iguana with missing toes.

Soto, G. (1996). *Too many tamales.* **New York: Putnam.**

Maria tries on her mother's wedding ring while making tamales. It disappears! Could it be in one of the 24 tamales that were made? This book is also available in Spanish as *Qué Montón de Tamales!*

BEHAVIOR 4

Elaborating on Ideas

- Adult elaborates on the child's ideas.
- Child spontaneously offers ideas about the story.

PARENT/CAREGIVER TIPS FOR BEHAVIOR 4

- When your child has an idea, stop and listen carefully.

- Try to understand your child's ideas.

- Encourage your child to tell you his or her ideas.

- Give your child a chance to talk about the story, and talk more about what your child has to say.

- Once you know what your child's ideas are, you can tell him or her what your ideas are, too.

Elaborating on Ideas

CLASS ACTIVITY

Extending a Story

 Purpose: To give the child a chance to offer ideas while reading the book and the adult a chance to elaborate on the child's ideas

Process:

1. Discuss ways to elaborate on the child's ideas.

2. Have the adult and child read *If You Give a Moose a Muffin*.

3. Have the adult encourage his or her child to talk about the story as it is being read.

4. As the adult reads, he or she should take the time to listen to the child when an idea is offered.

5. As the book is being read, the pair should repeat the moose's first request more than once.

6. The child should be asked to say a different thing that the moose might like.

7. The adult then can elaborate on it, and the pair can discuss their own story.

8. The adult can write down their ideas to share with the class.

9. At the conclusion of this activity, the "Paper Bag Puppet" activity could be sent home for discussion the following week.

Materials needed:

○ *If You Give a Moose a Muffin* by Laura Numeroff

○ paper

○ pen or pencil

○ _____

○ _____

○ _____

Elaborating on Ideas

TAKE-HOME ACTIVITY

Paper Bag Puppet

Purpose: To provide the child opportunities to talk about his or her ideas and the adult opportunities to elaborate on them

Process:

1. Read *Do You Want to Be My Friend?* to your child. (You can try creating similar activities with other books from the Recommended Books list.)

2. Talk about what animal would be a good friend for your child.

3. After you have talked about the animal your child picked to be his or her friend, make a paper bag puppet of this animal.

4. Write about your child's animal friend on the back of the puppet.

Materials needed:

○ *Do You Want to Be My Friend?* by Eric Carle

○ paper lunch bags

○ construction paper

○ scissors

○ crayons or markers

○ gluestick

○ _____

○ _____

○ _____

133

Elaborating on Ideas

Recommended Books

All of the books recommended for Behavior 4 are wonderful resources because they promote young children's thinking and provide opportunities for the child to discuss his or her self-generated ideas. Then, the adult has the opportunity to get into more detail about the ideas from the child.

Carle, E. (1988). *Do you want to be my friend?* **New York: Putnam.**

A young mouse goes out to look for a friend. He goes from animal to animal asking if anyone wants to be his friend. Read to find out who might want to be the mouse's friend.

Cousins, L. (2005). *Maisy dresses up.* **Cambridge, MA: Candlewick.**

What costume will Maisy wear to her friend Tallulah's party? Read along to find out what Maisy decides. This book is also available in Spanish as *Maisy Se Disfraza.*

Hill, E. (2000). *Where's Spot?* **New York: Penguin.**

Where is Spot? He's missing! The mother dog looks all over the house and finds many other animals before finally finding her puppy. This book is also available in Spanish as *¿Dónde Está Spot?*

Marshall, J. (1974). *George and Martha.* **Boston, MA: Houghton Mifflin.**

George and Martha are hippos and best friends. This book explores how friendship is maintained through acts of kindness and consideration.

Mayer, M. (1992). *There's a nightmare in my closet.* **New York: Puffin.**

A young boy scared of the nightmare in his closet must prepare to deal with it. When confronted with the nightmare, a whole different scenario emerges.

Numeroff, L. (1991). *If you give a moose a muffin.* **New York: HarperCollins.**

If you give a moose a muffin, he might want some jam. As the story progresses, the moose needs more to go with the things he already has. This book is also available in Spanish as *Si le Das un Panecillo a un Alce.*

Numeroff, L. (2000). *If you take a mouse to the movies.* **New York: HarperCollins.**

If you take a mouse to the movies, what will he need? Popcorn, of course! The mouse will need more as he is given more. This book is also available in Spanish as *Si Llevas un Ratón al Cine.*

Numeroff, L. (2002). *If you take a mouse to school.* **New York: HarperCollins.**

A boy takes his mouse to school. Of course, the mouse asks the boy for many things throughout the day. This book is also available in Spanish as *Si Llevas un Raton a la Escuela.*

Afterword

Let's Read Together: Improving Literacy Outcomes with the Adult–Child Interactive Reading Inventory (ACIRI) has demonstrated the importance of adults reading with their young children. Research is cited to support the notion that adults who use specific strategies that have been shown to be effective can help ensure their child's reading success when they enter school. We know this. What we have not known in the past is how to measure what occurs during interactive reading.

The ACIRI can provide the means of doing this. It can also inform teachers' instruction and assist them in planning effective interactive reading curricula for both adults and children. Funding has been drying up for many programs that work with families to assist them in learning these skills. One of the reasons for this is lack of sound assessment in this area. Funders keep giving money and seeing little in the way of solid results. Measurements of adult education skills and preschool skills do not capture what goes on during reading time together. For parents and caregivers to help their young children develop early literacy skills at home, research indicates that they must be able to give children guidance and teach them strategies that make sense. To help them do this, individuals who work with parents and caregivers need to know what parents are doing when they read with a child and how to help them improve. Results from the ACIRI can provide this information.

Cultural bias in tools is often discussed. The ACIRI measures skills that *all* children, regardless of their culture, need to master to become successful readers. These skills are easily adapted to any language and culture by using culturally congruent texts and activities. Wordless picture books can be substituted if families have low conventional literacy skills. Books can be used in any language, provided the person doing the testing understands the language and therefore the responses. Although no one instrument can claim to be perfect for all populations, individuals who use the ACIRI can work within diverse cultures in ways that make sense to them.

The ACIRI was designed to measure the interactive reading skills of both adults and children as they read together, and no claims are made that it can be used to provide individual literacy skills assessment for adults and for children separately. There are many published measures for that purpose. The uniqueness of this instrument is its ability to do something that hasn't been done before: simultaneously measure adult and child skills as they read together. After all, interactive reading should have an interactive assessment, shouldn't it?

References

Adams, M.J. (1990). *Beginning to read: Thinking and learning about print.* Cambridge, MA: MIT Press.

Armbruster, B., Lehr, F., & Osborn, J. (2003). *A child becomes a reader: Birth–preschool.* Washington, DC: National Institute for Literacy.

Baker, L., & Scher, D. (2002). Beginning readers' motivation in relation to parental beliefs and home reading experiences. *Reading Psychology, 23*(4), 239–269.

Belsky, J., & Cassidy, J. (1994). Attachment: Theory and practice. In M. Rutter & D. Hay (Eds.), *Development through life: A handbook for clinicians.* Oxford: Blackwell Science.

Bergin, C. (2001). The parent–child relationship during beginning reading. *Journal of Literacy Research, 22*(4), 681–706.

Billmeyer, R. (2003). *Strategies to engage the mind of the learner.* Omaha, NE: Dayspring Publishing.

Bowlby, J. (1973). *Attachment and loss: Vol. 2. Separation, anxiety, and fear.* New York: Basic Books.

Boyce, L.K., Cook, G.A., Roggman, L.A., Innocenti, M.S., Jump, V.K., & Akers, J.F. (2004). Looking at books and learning language: What do Latino mothers and young children do? *Early Education and Development, 15*(4), 371–385.

Brizius, J.A., & Foster, S.A. (1993). *Generation to generation: Realizing the promise of family literacy.* Ypsilanti, MI: High Scope Press.

Bus, A. (2001). Joint caregiver–child storybook reading: A route to literacy development. In S. Neuman & D. Dickinson (Eds.), *Handbook of early literacy research* (pp. 179–191). Baltimore: Guilford Press.

Bus, A.J., van IJzendoorn, M.H., & Pellegrini, A.D. (1995). Joint book-reading makes for success in learning to read: A meta-analysis on intergenerational transmission of literacy. *Review of Educational Research, 65*(1), 1–21.

Cairney, T.H. (2000). The construction of literacy and literacy learners. *Language Arts, 77*(6), 496–505.

Clark, M.M. (1976). *Young fluent readers.* London: Heinemann.

Clark, M.M. (1984). Literacy at home and at school: Insights from a study of young fluent readers. In H. Goelman, A.A. Oberg, & F. Smith (Eds.), *Awakening to literacy* (pp. 122–130). London: Heinemann.

Clay, M.M. (1979). *The early detection of reading difficulties: A diagnostic survey* (2nd ed.). Auckland, New Zealand: Heinemann.

Clay, M.M. (1985). *The early detection of reading difficulties* (3rd ed.). Auckland, New Zealand: Heinemann.

Clay, M.M. (1993). *An observation survey of early literacy achievement.* Auckland, New Zealand: Heinemann.

Clifford, G.J. (1984). Bach and Lesen: Historical perspectives on literacy and schooling. *Review of Educational Research, 54*(4), 472–500.

Cochran-Smith, M. (1984). *The making of a reader.* Norwood, NJ: Ablex.

Cochran-Smith, M. (1986). Reading to children: A model for understanding texts. In B.B. Shiefflin & P. Gilmore (Eds.), *The acquisition of literacy: Ethnographic perspectives* (pp. 35–54). Norwood, NJ: Ablex.

Cornell, E.H., Senechal, M., & Brodo, L.S. (1988). Recall of picture books by 3-year-old children: Testing and repetition effects in joint reading activities. *Journal of Educational Psychology, 80*(4), 537–542.

Crain-Thoreson, C., Dahlin, M.P., & Powell, T.A. (2001). Parent–child interaction in three conversational contexts: Variations in style and strategy. *New Directions for Child and Adolescent Development, 92,* 23–37.

DeBruin-Parecki, A. (1999, August). *The Adult/Child Interactive Reading Inventory: An assessment of joint storybook reading skills* (Tech. Rep. No. 2-004). Ann Arbor, MI: Center for Improvement of Early Reading Achievement.

DeBruin-Parecki, A. (2003). Evaluating adult/child interactive reading skills. In A. DeBruin-Parecki & B. Krol-Sinclair (Eds.), *Family literacy: From theory to practice*(pp. 282–302). Newark, DE: International Reading Association.

DeBruin-Parecki, A. (2004). *It's an open book! Using interactive reading to evaluate early literacy skills at home and at school.* Paper presented at the fifth annual CIERA Summer Institute, Ann Arbor, MI.

DeBruin-Parecki, A., & Oak, A. (2005, April). *Empowering teachers to use authentic assessment to inform their family and early literacy instruction.* Paper presented at the annual National Center for Family Literacy conference, Louisville, KY.

DeBruin-Parecki, A., Paris, S.G., & Seidenberg, J. (1997). Family literacy: Examining practice and issues of effectiveness. *Journal of Adolescent and Adult Literacy, 40*(8), 596–605.

De Castell, S., & Luke, A. (1983). Defining literacy in North American schools: Social and historical conditions and consequences. *Journal of Curriculum Studies, 15,* 373–389.

Dickinson, D.K., & Tabors, P.O. (Eds.). (2001). *Beginning literacy with language: Young children learning at home and school.* Baltimore, MD: Paul H. Brookes Publishing Co.

Durkin, D. (1966). *Children who read early.* New York: Teachers College Press.

Durkin, D. (1972). *Teaching young children to read.* Boston: Allyn & Bacon.

Edwards, P.A. (1991). Fostering early literacy through parent coaching. In E.H. Hiebert (Ed.), *Literacy for a diverse society: Perspectives, practices and policies* (pp. 199–213). New York: Teachers College Press.

Edwards, P.A. (1995). Combining parents' and teachers' thoughts about storybook reading at home and school. In L.M. Morrow (Ed.), *Family literacy: Connections in schools and communities* (pp. 54–69). Newark, DE: International Reading Association.

Edwards, P.A. (2004). *Children's literacy development: Making it happen through school, family and community involvement.* Boston: Allyn & Bacon and Pearson Education.

Elementary and Secondary Education Act of 1965, PL 89-10, 20 U.S.C. §§ 241 *et seq.*

Feldman, S. (2003). The right line of questioning. *Teaching PreK–8, 33*(4), 8.

Flood, J.E. (1977). Parental styles in reading episodes with young children. *The Reading Teacher, 30,* 864–867.

Genovese, E.D. (1974). *Roll, Jordan, roll: The world the slaves made.* New York: Pantheon.

Goals 2000: Educate America Act of 1994, PL 103-227, 20 U.S.C. §§ 5801 *et seq.*

Goodling, W.F. (1994). Giving kids an Even Start. *Principal, 74*(1), 24–25.

Guarino, D. (2004). *Is your mama a llama?* New York: Scholastic.

Guinagh, B.J., & Jester, R.E. (1972). How parents read to children. *Theory into Practice, 11*(5), 171–177.

Hansen, J. (2004). *"Tell me a story": Developmentally appropriate retelling strategies.* Newark, DE: International Reading Association.

Heath, S.B. (1983). *Ways with words: Language, life and work in communities and classrooms.* Cambridge, United Kingdom: Cambridge University Press.

Heath, S.B. (1986). What no bedtime story means: Narrative skills at home and at school. In B.B. Schieffelin & E. Ochs (Eds.), *Language socialization across cultures* (pp. 97–124). Cambridge, United Kingdom: Cambridge University Press.

Hiebert, E.H. (1981). Developmental patterns and interrelationships of preschool children's print awareness. *Reading Research Quarterly, 16*(2), 236–260.

Holdaway, D. (1979). *The foundations of literacy.* Sydney: Ashton Scholastic.

Howe, D., Brandon, M., Hinings, D., & Schofield, G. (1999). *Attachment theory, child maltreatment, and family support: A practice and assessment model.* London: MacMillan.

International Reading Association & National Association for the Education of Young Children. (1998). Learning to read and write: Developmentally appropriate practices for young children. *The Reading Teacher, 52*(2), 193–214.

Jordan, G.E., Snow, C.E., & Porche, M.V. (2000). Project EASE: The effects of a family literacy project on kindergarten students' early literacy skills. *Reading Research Quarterly, 35*(4), 524–546.

Kertoy, M.K. (1994). Adult interactive strategies: The spontaneous comments of preschoolers during joint storybook readings. *Journal of Research in Childhood Education, 9,* 58–67.

Klesius, J.P., & Griffith, P.L. (1996). Interactive storybook reading for at-risk learners. *The Reading Teacher, 49*(7), 552–560.

Lancy, D.F., Draper, K.D., & Boyce, G. (1989). Parental influence on children's acquisition of reading. *Contemporary Issues in Reading, 4*(1), 83–93.

Lionni, L. (1967). *Frederick.* New York: Dragonfly Books.

Martin, L.E. (1998). Early book reading: How mothers deviate from printed text for young children. *Reading Research Quarterly, 37*(2), 137–160.

Martin, L.E., & Reutzel, R.D. (1999). Sharing books: Examining how and why mothers deviate from print. *Reading Research and Instruction, 39*(1), 39–69.

Martinez, M. (1983). Exploring young children's comprehension through story time talk. *Language Arts, 60*(2), 202–209.

McCarthey, S.J. (2000). Home-school connections: A review of the literature. *Journal of Educational Research, 93*(3), 145–153.

McGee, L., & Richgels. D. (2003). *Literacy's beginnings: Supporting young readers and writers* (4th ed.). Boston: Allyn & Bacon.

Monaghan, E.J. (1991). Family literacy in early 18th-century Boston: Cotton Mather and his children. *Reading Research Quarterly, 26*(4), 342–370.

Morrow, L.M. (1983). Home and school correlates of early interest in literature. *Journal of Educational Research, 76*(4), 221–230.

Morrow, L. (1989). Using story retelling to develop comprehension. In K. Muth (Ed.), *Children's comprehension of text* (pp. 37–58). Newark, DE: International Reading Association.

Morrow, L.M. (1990). Assessing children's understanding of story through their construction and reconstruction of narrative. In L.M. Morrow & J.K. Smith (Eds.), *Assessment for instruction in early literacy* (pp. 110–133). Upper Saddle River, NJ: Prentice Hall.

Nash, A., & Hay, D. (2003). Social relations in infancy: Origins and evidence. *Human Development, 46*(4), 222–232.

National Education Goals Panel. (1995). *Goals report: Executive summary: Improving education through family–school–community partnerships.* Washington, DC: U.S. Department of Education.

Neuman, S. (1999). Books make a difference: A study of access to literacy. *Reading Research Quarterly, 34*(3), 286–311.

Neuman, S.B., Copple, C., & Bredekamp, S. (1999). *Learning to read and write: Developmentally appropriate practices for young children.* Washington, DC: National Association for the Education of Young Children.

Ninio, A., & Bruner, J. (1978). The achievement and antecedents of labeling. *Journal of Child Language, 5*(1), 1–15.

Paratore, J.R. (2003). Building on family literacies: Examining the past and planning the future. In A. DeBruin-Parecki & B. Krol-Sinclair (Eds.), *Family literacy: From theory to practice* (pp. 8–27). Newark, DE: International Reading Association.

Paratore, J.R., Melzi, G., & Krol-Sinclair, B. (1999). *What should we expect of family literacy? Experiences of Latino children whose parents participate in an intergenerational literacy project.* Newark, DE: International Reading Association.

Paris, A.H., & Paris, S.G. (2003). Assessing narrative comprehension in young children. *Reading Research Quarterly, 38,* 36–76.

Paulsen, G. (1993). *Nightjohn.* New York: Bantam Doubleday Dell.

Pearson, D., Roehler, L., Dole, J., & Duffy, G. (1992). Developing research in reading comprehension. In J. Samuels & A. Farstrup (Eds.), *What research has to say about reading instruction* (pp. 145–199). Newark, DE: International Reading Association.

Purcell-Gates, V. (2000). Family literacy. In M.L. Kamil, P.B. Mosenthal, P.D. Pearson, & R.J. Barr (Eds.), *Handbook of reading research* (Vol. III, pp. 853–870). Mahwah, NJ: Lawrence Erlbaum Associates.

Resnick, M.B., Roth, J., Aaron, P.M., Scott, J., Wolking, W.D., Larsen, J.J., et al. (1987). Mothers reading to infants: A new observational tool. *The Reading Teacher, 40*(9), 888–894.

Rogers, R. (2001). Family literacy and the mediation of cultural models. *National Reading Conference Yearbook, 50,* 96–114.

Roser, N., & Martinez, M. (1985). Roles adults play in preschoolers' response to literature. *Language Arts, 62*(5), 485–490.

Scarborough, H.S., & Dobrich, W. (Eds.). (1994). On the efficacy of reading to preschoolers. *Developmental Review, 14*(3), 245–302.

Senechal, M., Cornell, E.H., & Broda, L.S. (1995). Age-related differences in the organization of parent–infant interactions during picture-book reading. *Early Childhood Research Quarterly, 10*(3), 317–337.

Smolkin, L.B., & Donovan, C.A. (2002). "Oh excellent, excellent question!": Developmental differences and comprehension acquisition. In C. Block & M. Pressley (Eds.), *Comprehension instruction: Research-based best practices* (pp. 140–157). New York: Guilford.

Snow, C., Burns, M.S., & Griffin, P. (Eds.). (1998). *Preventing reading difficulties in young children.* Washington, DC: National Academies Press.

Sonnenschein, S., & Munsterman, K. (2002). The influence of home-based reading interactions on 5-year-olds' reading motivations and early literacy development. *Early Childhood Research Quarterly, 17*(3), 318–337.

Sperling, R.A., & Head, D.M. (2002). Reading attitudes and literacy skills in prekindergarten and kindergarten children. *Early Childhood Education Journal, 29*(4), 233–236.

St. Pierre, R.G., & Swartz, J.P. (1995). The Even Start Family Literacy Program. In S. Smith (Ed.), *Two generation programs for families in poverty: A new intervention strategy* (pp. 37–66). Norwood, NJ: Ablex.

Storch, S.A., & Whitehurst, G.J. (2001). The role of family and home in the literacy development of young children from low-income backgrounds. *New Directions for Child and Adolescent Development, 92,* 53–71.

Swift, M.S. (1970). Training poverty mothers in communication skills. *The Reading Teacher, 23*(4), 360–367.

Teale, W.H. (1978). Positive environments for learning to read: What studies of early readers tell us. *Language Arts, 55,* 922–332.

Teale, W.H. (1981). Parents reading to their children: What we know and need to know. *Language Arts, 58,* 902–912.

Teale, W.H. (1984). Reading to young children: Its significance for literacy development. In H. Goelman, A. Oberg, & F. Smith (Eds.), *Awakening to literacy* (pp. 110–130). Exeter, NH: Heinemann.

Trevarthen, C., & Aitken, K.J. (2001). Infant intersubjectivity: Research, theory, and clinical applications. *Journal of Child Psychology and Psychiatry, 42*(1), 3–48.

U.S. Census Bureau. (2006, March 16). *Estimated population of Michigan counties: 2000–2005.* Retrieved April 6, 2006, from http://www.michigan.gov/hal/0,1607,7-160-15481_28382-138587—,00.html

Vernon-Feagans, L., Hammer, C.H., Miccio, A., & Manlove, E. (2003). Early language and literacy skills in low-income African-American and Hispanic children. In S.B. Neuman & D.K. Dickinson (Eds.), *Handbook of early literacy research* (pp. 192–210). New York: Guilford Press.

Vygotsky, L.S. (1978). *Mind in society: The development of psychological processes.* Cambridge, MA: Harvard University Press.

Wasik, B.A., & Bond, M.A. (2001). Beyond the pages of a book: Interactive book reading and language development in preschool classrooms. *Journal of Educational Psychology, 93*(2), 243–250.

Whitehead, M. (2002). *Developing language and literacy with young children.* London: Paul Chapman Publishing.

Whitehurst, G.J., Epstein, J.N., Angel, A.M., Payne, A.C., Crone, D., & Fischel, J.E. (1994). Outcomes of an emergent literacy intervention in Head Start. *Journal of Educational Psychology, 86*(4), 541–556.

Whitehurst, G.J., Falco, F.L., Lonigan, C.J., Fischer, J.E., DeBaryshe, B.D., Valdez-Menchaca, M.C., et al. (1988). Accelerating language development through picture book reading. *Developmental Psychology, 24*(4), 552–559.

Wolfe, P., & Nevills, P. (2004). *Building the reading brain, PreK–3.* Thousand Oaks, CA: Corwin Press.

Yaden, D.B., Smolkin, L.B., & Conlin, A. (1989). Preschoolers' questions about picture, print, conventions and story text during reading aloud at home. *Reading Research Quarterly, 24*(2), 188–214.

Yetman, N.R. (1970). *Voices from slavery.* New York: Holt, Rinehart, & Winston.

Statistical Support
for the ACIRI

This appendix is designed to provide the reader with statistical support for the ACIRI. The ACIRI has been used around the country by a number of programs of various types. The data below are from the follow-up to the original pilot study. Following the original pilot study, the tool was revised based on teacher and parent comments and statistical results. The information presented here is based on data collected on the ACIRI. A discussion of the reliability and validity of the ACIRI also is provided. The data were collected at an Even Start program over a 2-year period.

Even Start is a federal demonstration project that provides both supportive and educational services to parents and children. Participants must have a child ranging in age from newborn to 7 years old to participate. The program has both at-home components and center-based components. Participants in the program (described next) spend the majority of the first 2 years receiving at-home visits from teachers and the following 2 years spending more time at the center in various capacities. The data for this study were collected in participants' homes.

GENERAL DESCRIPTION OF SITE

The site of this work was an Even Start program in the Midwest in an area that has experienced a large decline in employment over the last decade. The two school districts that feed into the program cover 32 square miles and include parts of five cities and two townships. This area contains the oldest housing in the county and has shown dramatic increases in the number of impoverished and at-risk families.

Approximately 45,000 people live in the area served, and each year about 90 of the highest risk families in the area are able to enter the program. The majority of families served are Caucasian. African Americans, Hispanics, Asian Americans, and Native Americans combined make up 20%–25% of the participants. The percentage of children in poverty ranges from 31% to 47%. Unemployment rates hover at approximately 10%. Five of the six local high schools have a drop-out rate of about 10%, the highest among the 21 county school districts. Five of the six local elementary schools qualify for Title I, and almost half of students are enrolled in Title I. The free or reduced lunch rates are approximately 60%.

Staff

At the time of the study, the teaching and administrative staff of the program consisted of three administrators (an adult literacy coordinator, an early child-hood coordinator, and a coordinator of community education/federal pro-grams, who oversaw all aspects of the program), five family support visitors (home-visiting teachers), and two family service workers (center support staff). They all were Caucasian women ranging in age from 37 to 54 years. Their edu-cational levels ranged from bachelor's degrees to master's degrees and some doctoral-level work. All degrees were in either education or social work, and all family support visitors were certified teachers with early childhood endorse-ments. All family support visitors and family service workers were with the program a minimum of 3 years. All administrators were with the program since its inception. All of the staff have children of their own.

Participants

Data for this study are available for 75 mothers and their children (see Tables A.1 and A.2). They were enrolled in the program either the first year of the study, the second year of the study, or both years. The ages of the adults ranged from 19 to 49 years, with the majority being in their mid- to late twenties. The children (approximately 50% boys and 50% girls) ranged in age from 2 to 7 years old, with the majority being 3 and 4 years old. Of the participating dyads, 13.3% were African American, 6.1% were Hispanic, 2.6% were Native American, 3.6% were of mixed ethnic heritage, and 74.4% were Caucasian.

Design

This study was designed to determine a) whether the ACIRI was sensitive to growth and change over time and b) whether teachers found the ACIRI useful as a measurement of adult and child reading behavior and progress. A fall measure was taken at the beginning of the program year in September, and a spring measure was collected at the end of the program year in May to offer insight about growth over time and usefulness of the tool. Time, developmen-

Table A.1. Sample by adult age

Age of adults	Frequency	Percentage
18–22	21	28%
23–29	37	49%
30–39	12	16%
40–49	5	7%
Total	75	100%

Table A.2. Sample by child age

Age of children	Frequency	Percentage
2	13	17%
3	20	27%
4	18	24%
5	14	19%
6–7	10	13%
Total	75	100%

tal changes, and varied curricula were expected to account for changes, and it was hoped that teacher comments during interviews and through questionnaires would shed light on the tool's usefulness.

Because the population was not large or stable enough to attempt to randomize or set up control groups, this study was not designed to be a controlled experiment. Between fall and spring, individual teacher instruction varied and was based on the literacy objectives of the program curriculum and behaviors on the ACIRI. For adults, these objectives included learning to provide relevant, functional, and meaningful language experiences for children; to focus on holistic approaches to communication skills; and to use printed materials as a source of learning and shared enjoyment. For children, the objectives were learning to understand speech and speaking, connect print to meaning, and gain knowledge about books and reading. Home-visiting teachers assisted families in reaching these objectives in various ways based on individual and family skill levels and needs.

Helping adults and children gain the skills that have been shown to promote academic success for children as they enter school was and is the overarching goal of this Even Start program. Many of the skills that have been demonstrated to be important for reaching this goal are those measured by the 12 items on the ACIRI. The ACIRI promotes improvement of interactive reading skills by providing an initial starting point for assessment and a guide to understanding where instructional emphasis should be placed. The ACIRI also allows for tracking the growth of joint reading behaviors over time.

RESULTS OF THE PILOT STUDY

Seventy-five pairs of adults and children were measured with the ACIRI in two waves of data collection, with 36 in the first year and 39 in the second year. Tables A.1 and A.2 present the sample by age of participating adults and children.

Among the 75 pairs, 13 participated in the ACIRI program twice and their data were collected in both waves. Compared with the whole sample, these 13 adults were younger, with 39% between 18 and 22 years old, and more of their children (46%) were 3 years old at the time of the first wave of data collection.

For each wave of data collection, two tests were administered to the paired participants: one prior to the program (pretest) and the other after the implementation of the program (posttest).

MAJOR FINDINGS

Reliability

Reliability tests were conducted for adult and child versions of the tool separately. Alpha coefficients were calculated for both pre- and posttests and for sub-scales and overall. As Tables A.3 and A.4 indicate, overall the tool for both adult and child versions was very reliable with alpha coefficients of .80 or above across time and versions. The category Promoting Interactive Reading

Table A.3. Reliability coefficients for the ACIRI, adult behaviors

Scale	Number of items	Reliability Pretest	Reliability Posttest
Enhancing Attention to Text	4	.59 (.64)	.30 (.86)
Promoting Interactive Reading and Supporting Comprehension	4	.74	.78
Using Literacy Strategies	4	.56	.68
Adult behavior total	12	.82	.80

Note: n = 75 for pretest, and n = 65 for posttest.

Table A.4. Reliability coefficients for the ACIRI, child behaviors

Scale	Number of items	Reliability Pretest	Reliability Posttest
Enhancing Attention to Text	4	.48 (.58)	.06 (.47)
Promoting Interactive Reading and Supporting Comprehension	4	.73	.80
Using Literacy Strategies	4	.61	.78
Child behavior total	12	.81	.81

Note: n = 75 for pretest, and n = 65 for posttest.

and Supporting Comprehension had the highest reliability among the subscales with coefficients ranging between .74 and .80. The category of Using Literacy Strategies had a better reliability in the posttests for both versions (.68–.78) compared with those for the pretest (.56–.61). However, the category Enhancing Attention to Text had a low reliability due to one of the four items: Adult gives the child an opportunity to hold the book and turn pages/Child holds the book and turns the pages on his or her own or when asked. With that item excluded, the reliability would go up to .64–.86 for the adult section, and .47–.58 for the child section. Overall, the corresponding scores for the paired adult and child are strongly correlated, as shown in Table A.5.

Table A.5. Correlation between adult and child behavior scores

Adult behavior	Enhancing Attention to Text Pre/Pre	Enhancing Attention to Text Post/Post	Promoting Interactive Reading and Supporting Comprehension Pre/Pre	Promoting Interactive Reading and Supporting Comprehension Post/Post	Using Literacy Strategies Pre/Pre	Using Literacy Strategies Post/Post	Total Pre/Pre	Total Post/Post
Enhancing Attention to Text	.88	.71						
Promoting Interactive Reading and Supporting Comprehension			.94	.95				
Using Literacy Strategies					.83	.80		
Total							.92	.90

Note: n = 75 for pretest, and n = 65 for posttest.

Interrater Reliability

Teachers participated in a number of workshops designed to instruct them in the use and purposes of the inventory. The scoring system was carefully defined, and the origins of all of the behaviors were discussed and explained. In addition, supporting literature was supplied. All teachers present were familiar with the literacy concepts represented in the ACIRI items. After a number of these training sessions, the ACIRI was piloted and examined for interrater reliability.

Interrater reliability was calculated among eight raters from a group consisting of program teachers, administrators, and community service workers. They watched three sets of dyads on videotape, each reading two books matched for difficulty and vocabulary level. Frequency counts of raters' scores across individual items were done for each dyad and each book to find how many of the raters scored each item the same. This provided the means of showing interrater agreement on each book for each dyad. A percentage of agreement was then calculated for each dyad. The percentage of agreement for all dyads and all books was then averaged, giving the total agreement figure. Having the same dyad read two different books also allowed for examination of the effect of varied materials on the scoring procedure. The "materials" reliability (two books by the same author read by the same dyad) was calculated with frequency counts of raters' scores on individual ACIRI items of the same dyad over two episodes reading matched books. The percentage of agreement across each matched pair was then figured. These three total percentages were then averaged, resulting in the total agreement figure.

The examination of the ACIRI for interrater reliability resulted in 97% agreement among eight raters across six observed reading dyads. When "materials" reliability was calculated for dyads who read two different books matched for author, vocabulary, and difficulty, raters agreed 99% of the time on scores for the pairs.

Validity

Construct Validity

Construct validity of an instrument is determined by examining the items on that instrument and determining if they are a fair and representative sample of the general domain that the instrument was designed to measure (American Educational Research Association [AERA], American Psychological Association [APA], & National Council on Measurement in Education [NCME], 1985). This is most often ascertained through reference to related research and theories. The behaviors (items) on the ACIRI are based on research and theory in the field of joint storybook reading, as reviewed in earlier chapters. The ACIRI does contain and measure those interactive reading behaviors that seem important to the development of literacy skills in children and the transfer of those skills to positive school outcomes. The author has also consulted and found additional support from the joint position statement on learning to read and write from the International Reading Association and the National Association for the Education of Young Children (1998) and the National Research Council Report, *Preventing Reading Difficulties in Young Children* (Snow, Burns, & Griffin, 1998).

Concurrent Validity

Concurrent validity of an assessment instrument is ascertained when scores on the newly designed instrument are compared with test scores on an already established instrument designed to measure the same constructs (AERA, APA, & NCME, 1985). It has not been possible to establish concurrent validity due to the unavailability at this time of any other instrument designed to measure interactive reading behaviors during storybook reading times. As noted previously, some instruments examine only adult behavior during interactive reading sessions with young children; however, until actual reading development of the child and instructional effectiveness of the adult can be measured jointly, verifying concurrent validity is problematic.

Consequential Validity

Consequential validity occurs when a designed instrument has positive consequences for those who use it. In the case of the ACIRI, this would mean that the implementation, concepts, and content of the ACIRI promote future improved interactive reading and learning experiences over time. Consequential validity has tremendous implications for newly developed authentic assessments such as the ACIRI.

> High priority needs to be given to the collection of evidence about the intended and unintended effects of assessments on the ways teachers and students spend their time and think about the goals of education. It cannot just be assumed that a more "authentic" assessment will result in classroom activities that are more conducive to learning. (Linn, Baker, & Dunbar, 1991, p. 17)

To provide evidence of consequential validity, the author offers the following excerpts about administration, purpose, and usefulness of the ACIRI taken from 1997–1998 interviews with the teachers who piloted and continue to use this tool. These comments address the positive implications of the ACIRI for both teaching and learning.

Teacher 1: After it's been done, I'll talk about some of the things like, "You did really well on this. One thing that I noticed you weren't doing that you might want to think about doing is…. And this is why this is important when you read to your children…." It really helps them stay focused on the story, and it makes them really think about more than just the words. They have to think about things they are doing while they read, and that's a good way to develop skills.

Teacher 2: The Adult–Child Interactive Reading Inventory is useful. A lot of the parents really enjoyed reading to their children for me, and *then afterward I told them, "Gee, you do this really, really well, and the only thing I see that you could do that you don't do is...." They were really happy to know those things and have been using them, as far as I can see—at least trying to utilize some of that information.*

Teacher 3: *It does help me at the beginning to know what behaviors to help with or to model. The ACIRI is not difficult to use. I don't have any problem with it. It kind of points out behaviors, like when I see parents who just read real blatantly and don't try to interact with the story and the child. They're just reading to read and get through. Those kinds of things I look for. Those are the kinds of things I model to start with. I don't take this and say, "You just don't do...." No, we don't do that. It's a key to me to know next week when I'm doing it to really exaggerate those behaviors. In that respect, the ACIRI is helpful.*

Teacher 4: *I think the Adult–Child Interactive Reading Inventory is helpful for initial diagnosis of joint reading behaviors. It's really helpful because I can say to a mom, "Do you notice that when you do this, this happens? Maybe if you try something else. Try this, and I don't think that will happen anymore." It really is good to have both of them there together. It's valuable as a teaching tool because I can always say to the mom, "You did really well. There are only one or two places where I think...." It gives me a jumping off place. This definitely provides valuable information to me and, I think, to the family members and administrators.*

Teacher 5: *I don't have a problem using the ACIRI. I don't think it's difficult to use. I feel that it's interesting to see, to watch the interaction between parent and child. As far as a teaching tool, there's usually a couple of things I'll address, a couple of suggestions I'll make after watching them read using prediction and relating it to their own experiences. I'll talk about that a little bit, helpful things for the parent. If there's a really poor relationship between the parent and child, I'll say in a nice way, "It's okay for him to want to turn the pages. You need to go a little faster. You don't have to read every single word. That's okay." The difficulty sometimes is that the parents are uncomfortable. We work to make that better. Other than that, the children love it. They love to be read to by their parents.*

It appears from these comments and others offered in more casual instances that teachers have found the ACIRI useful and feel it is accomplishing its purposes of being a teaching, learning, and evaluation tool that has positive consequences for adults, children, and teachers. Adults are able to discover the joint storybook reading skills they need to improve or learn and to get focused skill instruction from teachers. Children benefit by participating in interactive reading sessions and ultimately profit when their parent or guardian learns how to encourage the development of important literacy skills. The teachers gain information that allows them to design lessons that concentrate more closely on the skills that parents and guardians need to improve. This allows them to note strengths and provide recognition as opposed to teaching the same curriculum to everyone, risking participant boredom and lack of motivation.

DESCRIPTION OF SCORES

Tables A.6 and A.7 present the means of the total and three subscales of both pre- and posttests for adults and children, respectively. On a scale of 1–3, "Enhancing Attention to Text" had a high mean even at the pretest (2.08–2.10) with skewness to the left. "Promoting Interactive Reading and Supporting Comprehension" and the total score had means of approximately 1.5 with no evident skewness. "Using Literacy Strategies" had low means between .70 and .80 with skewness to the right.

Table A.6. Adult behavior scale score for pre- and posttest

	Mean (standard deviation)	
Scale	Pretest	Posttest
Enhancing Attention to Text	2.10 (.57)	2.41 (.47)
Promoting Interactive Reading and Supporting Comprehension	1.39 (.91)	1.58 (.94)
Using Literacy Strategies	.73 (.69)	.81 (.81)
Parent behavior total	1.41 (.61)	1.60 (.59)

Note: n = 75 for pretest, and n = 65 for posttest.

Table A.7. Child behavior scale score for pre- and posttest

	Mean (standard deviation)	
Scale	Pretest	Posttest
Enhancing Attention to Text	2.08 (.55)	2.41 (.43)
Promoting Interactive Reading and Supporting Comprehension	1.39 (.88)	1.70 (.92)
Using Literacy Strategies	.75 (.72)	.77 (.87)
Parent behavior total	1.41 (.59)	1.63 (.60)

Note: n = 75 for pretest, and n = 65 for posttest.

Gain Scores from Pre- to Posttests

Paired t tests were conducted to examine whether any change took place between pre- and posttests. As shown in Table A.8, the participating adults achieved significant gains in the total scores and one of the three subscores: "Enhancing Attention to Text." Like their paired adults, the participating children also gained significantly in the total score and "Enhancing Attention to Text," as indicated in Table A.9. In addition, the children achieved significant gains in "Promoting Interactive Reading and Supporting Comprehension."

Table A.8. Adult behavior scale score from pre- to posttest

	Mean		Statistical significance
Scale	Pre	Post	
Enhancing Attention to Text	2.12	2.41	$p < .01$
Promoting Interactive Reading and Supporting Comprehension	1.43	1.58	$p = .12$
Using Literacy Strategies	.71	.81	$p = .32$
Parent behavior total	1.42	1.60	$p < .01$

Note: Based on paired t test, n = 65.

Table A.9. Child behavior scale score from pre- to posttest

	Mean		Statistical significance
Scale	Pre	Post	
Enhancing Attention to Text	2.11	2.41	$p < .01$
Promoting Interactive Reading and Supporting Comprehension	1.41	1.70	$p < .01$
Using Literacy Strategies	.71	.75	$p > .05$
Child behavior total	1.41	1.63	$p < .01$

Note: Based on paired t test, n = 65.

Gain Scores by Children's Age and Repeated Training

Because the participants varied greatly in age and number of times they attended the program, regression analysis was conducted to investigate whether the gain score was related to the participants' age and repeated program participation. Given a strong negative correlation found between the gain and pretest scores in all of the categories (e.g., −.45 between pretest and gain in the total scores), which means that original high scorers gained less than the original low scorers after implementation of the program in general, the pretest score was also included in the regression analysis so that age effects or repeated program participation effects, if found, would not be confounded with the general pretest-status effects.

The results of regression analysis show that adult gain scores were predicted by age of the adults' paired children instead of their own age, whereas children's gains were not affected significantly by either their own or the paired adults' age. Table A.10 illustrates how adult gain scores were associated with the age of the adults' paired children. Significant gains were shown from pre- to posttests in all of the scores for adults whose paired children were age 3 years or younger; however, three of four gain scores were not significant for adults whose paired children were age 4 years or older. Based on the results of regression analysis, this adult-gains-by-child-age interaction effect was significant ($p < .05$) for literacy strategies and nearly significant ($.05 < p < .10$) for interactive reading and the total literacy behavior. "Enhancing Attention to Text" has no adult-gains-by-child-age interaction effect since the adult gains did not vary between those with younger children and those with older ones.

Table A.10.   Adult behavior gain score by child age

| Adult behavior | Adult score | | | | | | Adult gain by child age interaction |
| | Children 1–3 years old | | | Children 4–7 years old | | | |
	Pre	Post	p	Pre	Post	p	
Enhancing Attention to Text	2.03	2.38	< .01	2.15	2.44	< .01	p > .05
Promoting Interactive Reading and Supporting Comprehension	1.38	1.73	< .05	1.46	1.46	> .05	p = .07
Using Literacy Strategies	.63	.93	< .05	.79	.71	> .05	p < .05
Total	1.36	1.68	< .01	1.47	1.54	> .05	p = .07

Note: n = 30 for the adult group with children 1–3 years old, and *n* = 35 for children 4–8 years old.

As adult behavior is not likely to change without changes in an adult's life, the finding may suggest that the program intervention did have desirable effects on adult interactive reading behaviors. The adult-gain-by-child-age effect may imply that it is easier to make changes in adult reading behavior when children are very young. In addition to child age effect on gain scores, the regression analysis also found that repeated program participation made a significant difference on adult and child gain scores in literacy strategies.

Table A.11. Adult and child gain scores in literacy strategies by repeated program participation

| | Scored in literacy strategies | | | | | | Gain by repeated participation |
| | First-time participants | | | Second-time participants | | | |
Participants	Pre	Post	p	Pre	Post	p	
Adults	.68	.71	> .05	.97	1.50	= .07	p < .05
Children	.71	.66	> .05	.75	1.34	= .16	p < .05

Note: n = 57 for the first participation; n = 8 for the second participation.

As shown in Table A.11, "Using Literacy Strategies" showed almost no gains from pre- to posttest for the first-time participants (.68–.71 for adults and .71–.66 for children) whereas the gains were great for second-time participants (.97–1.50 for adults and .75–1.34 for children). Although the gains from pre- to posttest did not reach to $p < .05$ level of significance for the second-time participants, the difference in amount of gains for the first-time and second-time participants was such that a significant gain-by-repeated-participation effect was detected after controlling for adult and child age and pretest score. Given the general tendency of pretest-status effect (i.e., higher scorer in pretest usually gained less after treatment), this positive repeated participation effect was unique, which may suggest that more training times work efficiently for improving specific reading behaviors (e.g., literacy strategies).

CONCLUSION

The ACIRI has achieved its original purposes of being sensitive to growth and change over time and being useful to teachers as a measurement of adult and child reading behavior and progress. The data analysis showed that the total means of both the adult and child part of the ACIRI were significant at the .01 level, indicating that, overall, adults and children both improved over time. All category and individual behavior means increased from the premeasure to postmeasure for both adults and children. Several showed significant differences, including the "Enhancing Attention to Text" category, which was significant at the .01 level for both adults and children, and "Promoting Interactive Reading and Supporting Comprehension," which was significant at the .01 level for children.

Although differences in scores on behaviors were modest in many cases, there still were positive changes to report. A small sample size and lack of a direct instructional intervention could have had an impact on the size of these differences. However, it is important to consider reasons why reported positive changes in reading behaviors might have occurred. One reason might be that without a formal intervention, with just the implementation of the normal home visitor program, both children and adults changed the ways they read together to include more useful behaviors. Other reasons for these changes might be due to time alone or maturation of the child or better reading skills due to practice. Whatever the reasons for demonstrated changes in interactive reading behaviors, the ACIRI did reveal a sensitivity to them. Examination of the data indicates that the ACIRI appears to have positive consequences for participants and is a sensitive measure of improving reading behaviors over time.

In addition to the focus on ACIRI scorcs for evaluation purposes, the data collection process also was valuable. It provided teachers with opportunities to instruct adults in needed literacy skills and to interact with children in positive reading cpisodcs. The adults gained by learning where they most needed to improve their reading skills when sharing books with their children. While the Even Start program was able to compile useful data to report to their funders to help ensure continued financial support, teachers were able to focus on the teaching and learning aspects of the tool. Administrators were very excited about the educational aspects of the tool and also were delighted to find an instrument that provided useful and needed data for program evaluation purposes.

REFERENCES

American Educational Research Association (AERA), American Psychological Association (APA), & National Council on Measurement in Education (NCME). (1985). *Standards for educational and psychological testing.* Washington, DC: Author.

International Reading Association & National Association for the Education of Young Children. (1998). Learning to read and write: Developmentally appropriate practices for young children. *The Reading Teacher, 52*(2), 193–214.

Linn, R.L., Baker, E.L., & Dunbar, S.B. (1991). Complex performance-based assessment: Expectations and validation criteria. *Educational Researcher, 20*(8), 15–21.

Snow, C., Burns, M.S., & Griffin, P. (Eds.). (1998). *Preventing reading difficulties in young children.* Washington, DC: National Academies Press.

Family Literacy Programs Case Study

with Amy Oak

This case study is based on four family literacy programs that were held in diverse Muskegon County communities located in western Michigan. Muskegon County is historically a working-class area on the shores of Lake Michigan with a population of more than 170,000, according to the 2000 census (U.S. Census Bureau, 2006). The programs that sponsored each series included a Latino community center in the city of Muskegon, which is the largest population center in the county; a Head Start program in another very diverse neighborhood also in the city of Muskegon; a school-based early childhood center in the city of Muskegon Heights, a community that borders the city of Muskegon and has a 77% African American population; and a consortium of early childhood programs in Holton, a rural area with a 96% Caucasian population and a large number of families living in poverty.

Each of the school districts in these communities include buildings that have not made adequate yearly progress (AYP) based on the regulations of the No Child Left Behind Act of 2001 (PL 107-110). The regional educational service agency for the county, the Muskegon Area Intermediate School District (MAISD), is charged by the Michigan Department of Education with supporting these districts in making the necessary changes to achieve AYP. One of the strong roles taken by the MAISD is to lead and champion local early childhood collaborations. Michigan's governor, Jennifer Granholm, is also a strong advocate for the important role that parents play in their children's development. Governor Granholm created the Great Parents, Great Start (GPGS) initiative to support parents of children birth to 5 years in which she strongly encouraged all parents and early childhood programs to read to children at least 30 minutes each day. This idea was quickly embraced by the MAISD and other key agencies and served as the impetus of the family literacy series. The GPGS initiative provided a small grant to the MAISD to collaborate with local programs in providing direct services to parents. As a part of the grant requirements, one part of the money had to be used for programs with a clear focus group and pre- and postassessments to determine the success of the intervention.

The research and application work being done by Dr. DeBruin-Parecki with the ACIRI provided an assessment and curriculum model that was a perfect fit with the GPGS grant requirements, the needs of the local district, and the goals of the MAISD. Thus, the MAISD GPGS Family Literacy Project was launched.

The rest of this chapter outlines the process of developing and implementing these family literacy events and the very positive results of the programs. The intention is to provide other community groups with a framework on which to create their own ACIRI-based family literacy events.

FOUNDATIONS

The first step in implementing the GPGS Family Literacy Project was to train early childhood staff to use the ACIRI. Dr. DeBruin-Parecki was contracted to provide a 1-day training on the use of the ACIRI. The information provided in this book can assist family literacy programs in creating their own curricula linked to the ACIRI. Several local programs that served 3- to 5-year-olds and their families were invited to attend. Representatives from Head Start, the state's 4-year-old program, Michigan School Readiness Program (MSRP), tuition preschool and early childhood special education (ECSE), Even Start, and local social services agencies responded. In addition to the ACIRI training, Dr. DeBruin-Parecki also shared the structure she had used in creating and conducting various family literacy series. From this base, the planning began.

The second step in establishing the program was selecting participants. Families were chosen based on several factors: willingness to commit to a 6- to 8-week program, residence in a district that had schools that had not made AYP, and at least one child in the target group who was between 3 and 5 years old.

SERVICES AND SCHEDULES

Each local program followed a similar structure with variations based on unique community resources and needs; however, each program provided the following services for participating families at no cost to the families:

- Educational child care for all children in the family

- Nutritious meals served at each meeting

- Books corresponding to each week's tips sent home along with related family activities

- Supplies necessary to do all activities at the meetings and at home

- Transportation to and from the sessions (This service was provided in the more rural programs.)

Within each of the meetings of the series, a similar schedule was followed (see Figure B.1). Within the four series held in Muskegon County, start times varied from 5:30 PM to 6:30 PM, but all programs ran for $1^1/_2$ hours. Each meeting began with a community meal (usually 45 minutes) that included the parents or caregivers and all children in the family, not just the target child. All

6:30	Dinner and socializing
7:15	Welcome
	Families share reading experiences and take-home activities from previous sessions.
7:30	Children go to child care.
	Parents and caregivers participate in week's skill tips.
7:45	Target children return.
	Parents read new book to child.
	Take-home activity explained and distributed.
8:15	All children return.
	Family activity time
8:30	Thanks and good-bye song

Figure B.1. Sample schedule.

staff involved in the project also ate with the families. As evident from the positive and growing interaction among staff, parents or caregivers, and children, everyone eating together played an important part in building the trust that strongly supports a nurturing learning environment.

Some programs followed the meal with a welcome, introductions, and icebreaker or sharing of the prior session's take-home activity and book (15 minutes). This provided additional whole-group interaction and gave the families models of additional things that could be done with the take-home materials.

At this point, all of the programs sent the children, including the target children, to quality, educational child care. Some programs used their own staff to provide the child care with high school students as support; other sites used existing community center child care facilities. All sites made a special effort to ensure a positive experience for the children. In some situations, the activities were even coordinated with the book for the evening.

While the children were gone, the parents and caregivers participated in the lesson for the session (15–30 minutes). The brief, fun-filled tips of the week were reflective of the behaviors observed in the ACIRI. The final decisions of which behaviors to feature were made based on the preseries ACIRI results. The featured book was always read aloud by the staff and/or parent volunteers at least once, in part to support adults with low literacy skills.

After the lesson, the target child from each family returned from child care. Parents or caregivers then read to their child, paying attention to implementation of the skills previously presented (15 minutes). This time might also include an explanation of the take-home activity and distribution of all materials needed to effectively do the activity.

All of the children then returned from child care to participate in a family activity time (15 minutes). These activities included a range of possibilities: songs and games appropriate to all ages, simple craft projects, measuring cookie ingredients for an at-home baking project, and making tamales from already prepared ingredients.

Several of the sites included a specific song or closing ritual. As the series progressed, more interaction within and between families, as well as with staff, often lengthened the evening much to everyone's enjoyment.

LESSON CONTENT

The skills observed in the ACIRI were the foundation of the curriculum for the series.

Generally, the skills were presented in the following segments:

Lesson 1: All Enhancing Attention to Text behaviors, which include promoting and maintaining physical proximity, sustaining interest, and sharing the book

Lesson 2: Posing and soliciting questions and pausing to answer questions the child poses

Lesson 3: Pointing to pictures and words to assist the child in identification and understanding of story content

Lesson 4: Relating the book content and child's responses to personal experiences

Lesson 5: Identifying visual cues related to the story (e.g., pictures, repetitive words); asking the child to recall information from the story

Lesson 6: Soliciting predictions and elaborating on the child's ideas

Although the basic planning, including ordering books, often must be done before the ACIRI assessment is done, the plans must be readjusted based on the strengths and needs of the parents participating in the learning. Assessment was done prior to Lesson 1 and following Lesson 6.

Promoting Interactive Reading and Supporting Comprehension is an important skill that supports the goal for the adult to relate the book's content and the child's responses to personal experiences. The companion behavior for the child is to begin to relate the book's content to his or her own personal experiences. This is a foundational strategy in comprehension as the child progresses in school, often referred to as making text-to-self connections. The choice of the book is crucial to support this skill development. Although each situation is unique, more detailed examples of lessons and related activities that support the thinking and planning for various early literacy groups is offered next.

In this first example, all of the families were of Latino background with Spanish as their first language. Most of the families were originally from Mexico, with a few from other countries in Central America. The book chosen, *In My Family, En Mi Familia* (Garza, 1996), reflects the life experiences of many of the families of Mexican American heritage. It comprises a series of illustrations with a narrative of memories of the moment depicted. In the introduction, Garza remembered "being made to feel ashamed of our (Mexican American) culture" and further stated that, "My art is a way healing these wounds." During the lesson, a parent was invited to read the book and both staff and other parents role-played the children. The reader-parent gave the "children" many opportunities to share their connections with the text and to share their family stories. The depth of the sharing brought forth tears from one mother who was reminded of how much she missed some of her family still in Mexico. Parents then had an opportunity to choose a page in the book to read to a partner and share a corresponding story. Through this sharing, the parents or caregivers had a chance to experience the power of being connected to text through life experiences. This gave them a foundation for encouraging that kind of sharing as their child returned from child care and they read parts of the book to their child. To further incorporate the cultural connections, the family activity time was a simple circle dance that is often done at parties and family gatherings in Latino communities. The take-home activity also supported personal connection with text. Each family was given a simple disposable camera and a blank book titled, *In My Family/En Mi Familia*. Each family was invited to take photos of daily family events and write a description in Spanish and/or English to create a text that supported children in making connections between text and life experiences. The program offered to develop the film. Over the course of the following weeks, families brought in their completed *En Mi Familia* books. Everyone celebrated and enjoyed each book. Copies were made that could be sent to extended family members. This personal book was then added to the growing family library in each home.

Not every program has the homogeneity of participants found at this site. Another program that included families of African American, Hispanic, and European heritage decided that finding a book that reflected common personal experiences was better served by creating a common experience. To achieve this end, the staff provided a fun and purposeful activity by inviting the local fire department to the meeting. The families had the opportunity to interact with firefighters, experience the trucks close up, and receive family safety tips. The featured book sent home with each family was *Fighting Fires* (Simon, 2002). As this book was read and reread, adults could connect the text to the fire department visit and children could share their experiences to deepen their understanding of the book. This choice also incorporated other important aspects: The text is nonfiction and allows young children an enticing entry to the genre. The families also received good home safety information in a very relaxed atmosphere. The take-home activity was a coloring book with family fire safety tips that provided an opportunity to review the ideas presented in the session.

These two very different examples highlight the variety of effective lessons that can be developed when staff members tailor the program to fit the needs of the communities served.

RESULTS AND REFLECTIONS

The results of the four GPGS Family Literacy Project sessions can be viewed on several levels. The most obvious benefits were evident at each session. The sight of 10–20 parents reading with their 3- to 5-year-old snuggled in their lap or next to them is enough to warm the heart of anyone committed to the concept of family literacy. At each session, the laughter, interaction, sharing between families, and connections with staff in a warm and informal setting were proof that the structure of the programs was family friendly. At each site, parents requested continued sessions beyond the scheduled programs.

Another measure of the results was the comments from parents on surveys at the end of the series:

Families identified favorite books: "We enjoyed the fire trucks book best because it has cool stuff." They also appreciated the home smoke detectors sent home by the firefighters.

"It is a great opportunity to get with other families and learn how to enjoy reading with your children, so you can both benefit from reading to them."

"We liked the part when the kids came from play (child care) and then we would read to them. The song and dance was a good touch at the end."

"Literacy night is a good program to help parents introduce reading to their child. It's good for the children to get to read, too, and then they learn how to act and listen while you read."

In response to a question about favorite take-home activities one parent wrote, "To be honest, Brandon really enjoyed the cookie mix. It was a pleasure making the cookies with a 4-year-old!"

Teachers often commented on the improved relationships with the families. They also observed that the specific skills were being incorporated in their own reading aloud to their classes as they became more aware of the value of involving the children. The information was shared on a more informal level with parents visiting the class, in-home visits, and single-session family literacy events. Several teachers became aware that they were being much more concrete with their suggestions as they encouraged parents not only to read with their children but also how to read with their children. One of the best summaries of the affective results was a 4-year-old boy returning from child care announcing in an enthusiastic way as he ran to his mother, "It's time for you to read to me now!"

Educational decisions cannot be made on only affective and observational data. The ACIRI provides the means to give quantitative information so important in this era of accountability. Using this lens, each of the four programs was successful in giving parents and children the experience necessary for them to improve the interactive nature of the read-aloud time.

RESULTS FROM THE ACIRI

The Muskegon program consisted of 56 families. Complete data were collected on 25 families. The children's mean age was 3 years, 10 months. The adults' mean age was 29 years, 6 months. Educational level of participating adults varied widely starting at an elementary level and ending at a college degree. Tables B.1 and B.2 show the quantitative results achieved on the ACIRI. Clearly, improvement occurred at the completion of the program.

IMPLICATIONS FOR FUTURE
PROGRAMS AND LESSONS LEARNED

After planning and implementing the four local family literacy programs, staff shared some common reflections on possible next steps and improvements about what happened in their programs. Some are big-picture next steps, and some are the details that can make a good program even better. The following issues are being pondered:

Table B.1. ACIRI adult category scores from pre- to posttest

Categories	Mean		Statistical significance
	Pre	Post	
Enhancing Attention to Text	1.73	2.65	$p < .01$
Promoting Interactive Reading and Supporting Comprehension	1.49	2.17	$p < .01$
Using Literacy Strategies	.67	1.68	$p < .01$
Parent behavior total	1.30	2.17	$p < .01$

Note: Based on paired t test, $n = 25$; Score range 0–3.

Table B.2. ACIRI child category scores from pre- to posttest

Categories	Mean		Statistical significance
	Pre	Post	
Enhancing Attention to Text	1.57	2.46	$p < .01$
Promoting Interactive Reading and Supporting Comprehension	1.29	2.00	$p < .01$
Using Literacy Strategies	.65	1.45	$p < .01$
Child behavior total	1.17	1.97	$p < .01$

Note: Based on paired t test, $n = 25$; score range 0–3.

- Mentoring between families could be supported and highlighted. Many parents were incorporated into the lessons informally, which could be done in a more systematic and effective manner. For example, parents from one series could be a part of the team that plans and delivers another series.

- Planning an advanced series for parents who wanted extended learning. Other parenting skills and community resources could be incorporated into the sessions.

- Expanding the sponsoring organization to reach beyond school and centers and include more social services agencies

- Designing eight sessions in the series instead of six would be far better to allow for a more complete introduction and night of preassessment. At the end of the program, a graduation celebration and postassessment could occur. Doing the pre- and postobservations during home visits was the original plan, but it wasn't always feasible.

- Using preassessment ACIRI data to modify the content of the lessons could make the teaching more focused and could be the basis for including parents as models of skill areas that are their strengths.

- Improving follow-up with parents and children could possibly include reunions and following the beginning reading development of the children.

The ACIRI is a very useful tool because it has multiple purposes. It can be used as an assessment to report data to funders and responsible agencies. It acts as a teaching and learning tool for parents/guardians, their children, and teachers. It provides a feasible, sensible framework for creating a program designed to improve adult–child interactive reading skills, skills that can predict a child's later success in school as a reader.

REFERENCE

Garza, C.L. (1996). *In my family, En mi familia.* San Francisco: Children's Book Press.
No Child Left Behind Act of 2001, PL 107-110, 115 Stat. 1425, 20 U.S.C. §§ 6301 *et seq.*
Simon, S. (2002). *Fighting fires.* New York: Scholastic.

APPENDIX C

Helpful Books and Web Sites

BOOKS FOR PARENTS/CAREGIVERS

Bettelheim, B. (1989). *The uses of enchantment: The meaning and importance of fairy tales.* **New York: Vintage.**

Discusses the importance of teaching children fairy tales. Explains how fairy tales engage, enlighten, and educate children, as well as stimulate their emotions.

Burns, M.S., Griffin, P., & Snow, C.E. (Eds.). (1999). *Starting out right: A guide to promoting children's reading success.* **Washington, DC: National Academies Press.**

Based on the Committee Report on the Prevention of Reading Difficulties in Young Children, this book provides information about what parents can provide to all children so they are prepared for reading instruction when they enter school.

Butler, D. (1998). *Babies need books: Sharing the joy of books with children from birth to six.* **Portsmouth, NH: Heinemann.**

Discusses the significance of reading, as well as provides synopses of books appropriate for different age ranges.

Codell, E.R. (2003). *How to get your child to love reading: For ravenous and reluctant readers alike.* **Chapel Hill, NC: Algonquin Books of Chapel Hill.**

A compilation of hundreds of creative ideas, projects, and suggestions that have been proven to encourage children birth through 8th grade to read more. Examples include mad-scientist experiments, storytelling festivals, and book-related crafts.

Fox, M. (2001). *Reading magic: Why reading aloud to our children will change their lives forever.* **San Diego: Harcourt.**

Describes the intense emotional impact that reading aloud has on children. Fox offers advice and activities for the most effective ways to read to children, such as the right books to choose and how to deal with problems that arise while children are learning how to read.

163

Leonhardt, M. (1993). *Parents who love reading, kids who don't: How it happens and what you can do about it.* **New York: Crown.**

Suggests ways to motivate reluctant readers. Offers tips for how poor readers can deal with problems in school as well as distractions. Leonhardt also provides an extensive list of child-recommended reading.

Trelease, J. (2006). *The read-aloud handbook* **(6th ed.). New York: Penguin.**

A guide for how to turn children into avid readers. Explains what reading aloud does for a child's imagination, how to choose the right books to read, and how to make reading more attractive than playing video games or watching television.

BOOKS FOR TEACHERS

Beaty, J.J. (1996). *Building bridges with multicultural picture books: For children 3-5.* **Upper Saddle River, NJ: Prentice Hall.**

Provides tips for how to choose appropriate multicultural picture books and how to introduce them into an early childhood program.

Burns, M.S., Griffin, P., & Snow, C.E. (Eds.). (1999). *Starting out right: A guide to promoting children's reading success.* **Washington, DC: National Academies Press.**

Based on the Committee Report on the Prevention of Reading Difficulties in Young Children, this book provides information and resources for teachers to assist them in ensuring that *all* children are prepared for reading instruction when they enter schools.

MacHado, J.M. (2002). *Early childhood experiences in language arts: Emerging literacy.* **Clifton Park, NY: Thomson Delmar Learning.**

Research and practice come together in creating the foundation for how planned programs affect children's language development. Offers examples and activities.

Neuman, S.B., Copple, C., & Bredekamp, S. (2000). *Learning to read and write: Developmentally appropriate practices for young children.* **Washington, DC: National Association for the Education of Young Children.**

Recommends ways for parents and teachers to support children's literacy development.

Neuman, S.B., & Roskos, K.A. (1998). *Children achieving: Best practices in early literacy.* **Newark, DE: International Reading Association.**

The focus is on theory and practice that is appropriate for children between 2 and 8 years old. The text discusses issues dealing with the varying needs of diverse children in regard to literacy and how to meet their needs. Each chapter focuses on a specific issue, what is already known about it, and how to address the issue.

Tabors, P.O. (1997). *One child, two languages: A guide for preschool educators of children learning English as a second language.* **Baltimore: Paul H. Brookes Publishing Co.**

Guidance on how to create a nurturing environment for English-language learners, monitor their progress, and create open communication with parents. Also stresses the importance of maintaining the children's native language and culture.

USEFUL WEB SITES FOR PARENTS/CAREGIVERS AND TEACHERS

Arthur (PBS Kids)

http://www.pbs.org/wgbh/pages/arthur

Child focused. Great web site with games and printables about the TV show *Arthur.*

Between the Lions: Get Wild About Reading

http://pbskids.org/lions

Child focused. This section offers games, printables, stories, and songs from the television show *Between the Lions.*

Between the Lions Parents & Teachers

http://pbskids.org/lions/parentsteachers

Parent and teacher focused. This section offers the same information that is on the homepage as well as literacy resources and information about the show.

Children's Technology Review

http://www.childrenssoftware.com

Reviews of child-focused software.

Family Education

http://www.familyeducation.com

Family focused. Offers parenting advice such as how to help your kids with homework, printable activities, and nutrition advice. Games and activities for grades pre-K through grade 12, advice on family life, and entertainment suggestions.

Gryphon House

http://www.ghbooks.com

Lists of activity books, children's literature, and bilingual books.

Ivillage: Pregnancy & Parenting

http://parenting.ivillage.com

Tips cover a wide range of issues that parents face. Articles and advice on many topics such as learners with attention deficit disorder and attention-deficit/hyperactivity disorder; infants, toddlers, and preschoolers under individual categories; and reading-focused learning activities. A calendar of activities can be found at http://parenting.ivillage.com/familytime/calendar/frame, which provides a new and different activity for each day of the month.

Jan Brett

http://www.janbrett.com

The many activities on Jan Brett's web site—including color pages, paper crafts, games, and more—are based on her many children's picture books such as *The Mitten* and *Gingerbread Baby*. The web site also provides "Classroom Help-a-longs" such as flash cards for reading and math.

KidSource Online

http://www.kidsource.com

Family focused. Offers a wide variety of information for all age groups on such topics as recreation, health, and organizations. Also a helpful section on products that have been recalled.

Kidspace at the Internet Public Library

http://www.ipl.org/div/kidspace/browse/rzn2000

A home of multiple interactive children's storybooks.

Maya and Miguel

http://pbskids.org/mayaandmiguel

Child focused. This section offers bilingual English and Spanish stories and activities.

Maya and Miguel: Parents & Teachers

http://pbskids.org/mayaandmiguel/english/parentsteachers/index.html

Parent and teacher focused. This section offers activities, lesson plans, and resources in English and Spanish.

National Association for the Education of Young Children

http://www.naeyc.org

Resources and tools about early childhood development that can be used in classrooms and programs.

Patricia Polacco

http://www.patriciapolacco.com

Author's web site with information on new books being published, appearances she'll be making, and activities for kids.

PBS TeacherSource

http://www.pbs.org/teachersource

Teacher focused. Information on arts, health, math, science, social studies, and pre-K. It also gives TV listings for educational programming and articles on how to use information in the classroom.

Pre-K Smarties: Teach Your Children

http://www.preksmarties.com/reading

Parent focused. Suggests links to other web sites as well as articles on a variety of topics such as gifted children and fun activities.

Reading Rockets

http://www.readingrockets.org

Parent, family, and teacher focused. Provides comprehensive information about reading, including strategies, children's books, research, lesson ideas, and more. Also accessible in Spanish.

Ready to Learn

http://www.pbs.org/readytolearn

Comprehensive web site that has sections for adults, teachers, and children and that offers resources, lesson plans, activities, information, and more.

Sesame Workshop

www.sesameworkshop.org/parents

Parent focused. Activities and advice from Sesame Street.

http://www.sesameworkshop.org/sesame street

Child focused. This section offers games, stories, art, and music.

Seussville University

http://www.randomhouse.com/seussville/university

Child focused. Dr. Seuss games that focus on reasoning, math, science, and reading.